I get asked to review a lo
this one. Janine offers a f

We won't reach this present generation of kids with yesterday's strategy. Here's a current strategy to reach today's kids. I highly recommend this book.

JIM WIDEMAN
Family Minister Pioneer, Jim Wideman.com

When you See Fireflies is filled with relevant and timely information about Generation Alpha, the children we are ministering to right now. It will equip you to understand who they are, why so many are leaving the church, and how to help this generation develop lifelong faith in Jesus. This book is a treasure trove for those in children's ministry as well as parents, educators, and even grandparents.

DR. JOSH MULVIHILL
Author and Executive Director, Renewanation.org

When you read Janine's book, you are convinced of four things: (1) She understands and models grace even in the way she encourages others, (2) She knows children and the challenges in teaching them having had years of experience, (3) She knows how times have changed and is forward thinking in her approach, (4) She recognizes the need for a clear presentation of the gospel. Anyone, particularly those working with children, would be helped by what God, wisdom, and experience have taught her.

DR. R. LARRY MOYER
Founder & CEO, EvanTell

I am so impressed with this book! Janine has looked and seen the fireflies. She knows it's time for us to take action, and she wants to call the church to see and respond as well. Get a highlighter ready—there are so many nuggets of helpful truth in this book; it's one of those books you can go back to again and again and still find more to chew on. Not only is it full of fantastic research and insight, it provides practical and considerate steps for implementing change. Wow! This book is now on my 'highly recommend' list!

SEAN SWEET
Preteen Pastor
Community Director, FourFiveSix.org

When You See Fireflies is a book that can help you reach today's kids and families. You'll get an eye-opening look at how today's children and parents are wired and how you can best connect with them. I recommend this book to anyone who wants to take your children and family ministry to the next level and impact people for Christ.

DALE HUDSON
Founder, Building Children's Ministry

When You See Fireflies is a top-shelf resource for ministry leaders! The powerful yet simple analogy that Janine uses guides any leader of children's ministry to consider why and how we are leading these next generations especially this newest generation, the Alphas. We are seeing such an incredible change in values and beliefs that we must ask tough questions and make deep changes if we are going to help children to become resilient in their own faith. The Alphas are here and coming into our ministry ready or not!

This is a thought-provoking read and one that any leader whether new or well-seasoned should spend some time thinking through. I highly recommend this resource to each and every leader.

TOM BUMP
Speaker, Ministry Coach,
Founder of RestoringLeaders.org
Author, *Valleys Over Mountains: A Guide Through the Hard Seasons*
Host, "The Kids Ministry Collective"
Podcast and Facebook Group

I love this book—for several reasons! In When You See the Fireflies, Janine McNally's writing voice is a combination of practitioner, child advocate, and futurist. As you read, you will not only discover a strong analysis of the challenge the church currently faces to raise resilient child disciples—but you will also discover a compilation of excellent research combined with the gathering of the voices of rising leaders in child discipleship and suggestions for innovative best practices for the challenging, and sometimes, dark times in which we live. Highly recommended as a great read and discussion starter for every church today.

VALERIE BELL
Awana CEO/Emerita
Author, *Resilient: Child Discipleship and the Fearless Future of the Church*

My colleague, Janine McNally, has put so much research, prayer, and heart into her new book *When You See Fireflies*. You can feel her passion and urgency for this generation of children, suffering as never before from anxiety, depression, uncertainty, and loneliness. Janine issues a poignant wakeup call to parents and to the church universal to shine a light, calling children "home" out of a very dark world. Important information for anyone who has children and/or ministers to children.

Dr. TRISHA PEACH
Author, *Your Children's Ministry from Scratch*

When You See Fireflies is a WAKE-UP CALL not only to Children's Ministry Leaders, but for Lead Pastors as well. It is a bold, fearless reality check on the cultural dusk that has settled upon our culture and reveals what it is going to require of ministries to be a Light in the Darkness that has stopped creeping and started storming into the schools, homes, and minds of our kids today. But it does more than just sound the alarm; it offers practical strategies for those who are willing to think differently so we can reach the next generation for Christ. Janine's book is going to play a major role in helping the church make the necessary shift it must in the years ahead.

KARL BASTIAN
Children's Pastor and Founder, Kidology.org

I love this invaluable resource Janine has gifted to the body of Christ. Effectively communicating the truth of the gospel to the next generation has never been more important. Janine is not afraid to confront the taboo topics that the church has historically avoided. Instead, she challenges the reader to face these controversial topics head-on so that a generation might be reached. In a world filled with distractions, Janine gives us the perfect blueprint on how the church can address these critical topics that directly affect the lpha generation.

ESTHER MORENO
Founder, Child's Heart LLC

WHEN YOU SEE FIREFLIES

EQUIPPING LEADERS AND PARENTS TO MINISTER EFFECTIVELY TO GENERATION ALPHA

JANINE MCNALLY

When You See Fireflies
Equipping Leaders and Parents to Minister Effectively to Generation Alpha

Published by Grace Theology Press in Houston, TX
www.GraceTheology.org

ISBN: 978-1-957202-04-4
eISBN: 978-1-957202-05-1

Special Sales: Most Grace Theology titles are available in special quantity discounts. Custom imprinting or excerpting can also be done to fit special needs. Contact Grace Theology Press.

DEDICATION

This book is dedicated to the following people:

My husband

He has always believed in me. Before I met him, I didn't know what it felt like to be unconditionally loved. Sure, I knew that God loved me unconditionally, and no one could love me more. But my husband was the human expression of the arms of God, wrapped around me, teaching me that I was valued and loved. Even as I launched my new ministry, Grace4Kidz, and began my doctorate, he believed in me and was my motivating force.

My children

Hannah—thank you for being my grammar editor and second-in-line encourager. Your friendship means the world to me, and I am so thankful for the transition we have finally made from child to best friend!

Jonathan—you make me so proud as I watch your amazing work ethic and your compassion for the less fortunate. Your generosity and loyalty stand as an amazing example to those around you!

Jami—we could never have imagined how wonderful it would be to have a later-in-life "surprise." It has been incredible to watch you blossom into an adventurous and bold young woman who loves the Lord.

All those who work with "Generation Alpha"

Lastly, I'd like to dedicate this book to those who lead and work in children's ministry. You are the unseen and unsung heroes of the church, laboring for an audience of One among the most precious and vulnerable population—our children. My prayer is that this book will be an encouragement and source of information to you as you share the love and sacrifice of Jesus with the youngest members of our churches and communities.

Contents

PART THREE
HELP: Change the Plan

PART FOUR
HOPE: Call Them In

Foreword

Many of us feel strong emotions when reflecting on our childhood. It may have been idyllic, with laughter and smiling family memories. Perhaps it was mediocre at best, with turn-key parents and the occasional forgotten permission slip. Worse still it might be painful, a place that we try to revisit as infrequently as possible. For me, one of the first things that comes to mind is the innocence of the world I grew up in, compared to the darker world into which I'm preparing to welcome my twin boys.

My brother and I often spent the spring and summer nights in Southern New Jersey playing in our backyard, loving the coolness of the evening, and chasing fireflies. We were enamored with catching and releasing as many as possible, and tracking them by their distinct glow. We'd often ask my mother when we needed to be back inside to prepare for bed, and her response would be "when you see fireflies". It's a phrase that represents the innocence of my childhood in such a big way. There was no cellphone to quickly 'check the time' or the technology stifling every waking moment. In many ways, I've grown up in a time where I feel as though I watched the world change, arguably for the worse, all due to the pressures and change that technology and social media have brought into our lives. I'm not doubting the benefits, but I think we forget that the benefits do not always outweigh the negatives.

Mom loved the idea of using my "fireflies" analogy for the title of this book, because her goal was to capture this very point. I've watched her dedicate herself to children's ministry over the years, passionate about keeping Jesus' love and the message of salvation simple, free, and clear.

We must face that the world is changing, and kids today are changing right along with it. Our approach and methods must follow suit, because if you try to tell a child today to measure time by seeing fireflies, they'll likely ask you if that's a new app on their phone!

I hope this book provides you with new ideas for your children's ministry, and that you allow yourself to examine your own approach for areas that could benefit from some change—because I promise you that today's kids will be better for it. You may find yourself teaching my boys one day, or any number of other children, and I hope your goal is the same as Mom's—to keep Jesus' love timeless and attainable in a world clamoring to share anything but Him.

Hannah (McNally) Fordred, MSPAS, PA-C,
DHEd Candidate

DOWNLOAD THE AUDIO BOOK FREE!

READ THIS FIRST

Just to say thanks for buying my book, I would like to give you the Audio Book version 100% FREE!

TO DOWNLOAD, GO TO:

http://grace4kidz.org/fireflies/AudioBook

1

Introduction: "When You See Fireflies"

Did you ever catch a firefly in a jar when you were a kid? They weren't very common in Australia where I grew up, so when I first visited the countryside here in the United States and saw those first tiny flashes of light, it was amazing. The seemingly insignificant glow of light shone brightly against the dark backdrop of the night. Each only lasted for a few seconds and then another one would light up, followed by more. Soon, I was surrounded by a cloud of little lights illuminating the darkness.

My husband calls them "lightning bugs," and there are other names, too, but our kids loved to chase them, and managed on occasion, to catch a few in a jar.

A number of years ago, we were living on two acres, which was surrounded by farm land in Pennsylvania. It was a warm summer evening and our two oldest kids asked if they could play outside for a while.

"When do we have to come back in?" they wanted to know.

We told them, "When you see fireflies."

We knew they would be completely absorbed with their childish antics and that a time deadline would be ineffective, and probably ignored, when competing with their fast-moving play. What would capture their attention?

"When you see fireflies."

Once dusk began to fall, they could be clearly seen. There would be no mistaking the time or making excuses. Each evening, for a short time, the fireflies would light up our entire backyard. Even in the midst of being completely absorbed with their fun, the little lights were impossible to miss. We knew that they would understand what we meant. It's time to come in.

"When you see fireflies."

We knew the environment—our yard was the perfect habitat. Fireflies need a specific, temperate climate. Many live in marshes or in wet, wooded areas where their larvae have abundant sources of food, plenty of leaf litter and underground burrows, clean water, diverse native vegetation, and dark nights. That was our backyard. The perfect environment. We knew our kids would be having fun, totally distracted, but their attention would be immediately grabbed by the little glowing lights flashing around them.

"When you see fireflies."

It was time. Dusk was falling and night was approaching. The fireflies were a familiar sight on our warm summer evenings. When they lit up, our kids knew it was time to come in. It was time to change direction. Their light signaled that it was time to stop what they were doing, listen, and come inside.

"When you see fireflies."

It was the perfect answer to their question. "When should we come inside?" We had their best interests at heart. Nighttime is no time for child's play. All kinds of dangers lurk in the darkness. It was time for them to follow our instruction. The message would be clear, effective, and impossible to miss. It was time to come inside.

Our world has become much darker now. We desperately need the kids and their families to hear the call.

"Come inside where it's safe."

The world is rapidly becoming bleaker as the generations race by, yet they seem to be running towards the night. Sadly, "playtime" needs to stop.

What message do we give? How do we capture their attention when there are so many distractions? So many diversions exist at every turn, even as near as their back pockets. How do we convince them that there is a better life that awaits them, one which is protected by the Almighty King of Kings and more meaningful than the world would ever be? How do we protect them from the dangers lurking in the dark?

We need to understand our kids and the world in which they are playing. We must proclaim a message that grabs their attention—one that they understand and that will break the magnetic attraction of the increasingly dark world. We must help them to experience God for themselves. We must restore the trust that people once had in the church. We must understand and adapt the call to their lives if we want to be relevant and effective. And we must do it now before it's too late.

"When you see fireflies."

PART ONE

HALT: It's Dark Outside

Fireflies can't be seen during the daytime. Their lights flash at dusk, as darkness begins to fall. Against the backdrop of nighttime, their little flashes glow brightly.

These insects live in a variety of warm tropical environments as well as in more temperate regions, and are a familiar sight on summer evenings. They fly around, often at head level, and our kids loved to run into the cloud of lights and watch them scatter.

Fireflies love moisture and often live in humid regions of Asia and the Americas. In drier areas, you will find them in marshes or in wet, wooded areas where their larvae have abundant sources of food (like snails and slugs, which they inject with a numbing fluid), plenty of leaf litter and underground burrows, clean water, diverse native vegetation, and dark nights.

The right environment. Dark nights. I used to tell our children that the worst things happen at night. As our country and world continue to change, the "nights" are growing darker and longer. It's time for our children to stop playing.

Halt! It's dark outside.

2

What a Wonderful World? It's Getting Darker

In 1967, at the height of the Vietnam war, Louis Armstrong recorded a single that would go on to become one of the most beloved songs of all time. Armstrong sang about babies. He realized that they would learn more than he would ever know.

It's obvious to most of us that our children have out-learned us in so many ways. We might have greater wisdom, but their knowledge is outpacing us! Armstrong believed in a wonderful world, and perhaps it is, from certain viewpoints, but the way I see it, it's not so wonderful anymore. Of course, there is endless beauty in God's creation. But today, in terms of morality and truth, it seems like we are living at a time of ever-increasing struggle and pain, while the world around us becomes progressively darker.

Our youngest daughter, Jami, currently attends a Christian university and is a member of Generation Z (1997-2010). Even though she is surrounded by students who love the Lord, she regularly shares stories of the struggles that are all too common amongst her fellow classmates—stories of pain, anxiety, self-harm, and even thoughts of suicide.

So many stories.

So many young people trying to cope, trying to survive. When speaking with her a little while ago, I asked her why she thought so many of her friends were struggling. Her answer was, "Mom, look at the world we are growing up in."

As I think about her response, her point is well taken. Do you ever look around the world and wonder how everything became such a mess?

When I was young, I remember my grandparents telling us stories of the world they grew up in. It all seemed so foreign.

I remember when we purchased our very first "black and white" television, a brand-new invention. Entertainment was at our fingertips with just the press of a button. It was amazing!

Not too many years later, the first computers arrived. I remember being so proud of my first laptop. It had a floppy drive and must have weighed close to 30 pounds, but I loved it.

A few years later along came the internet. I remember the very first email I sent to my family in Australia. I said to my husband, "I can't believe that sentence has already travelled across to the other side of the world." It was a time of exciting and rapid change.

When comparing that past era to our world today, it's difficult to imagine a more confusing time.

Not only has technology continued to develop at an unbelievably fast pace, the staggering moral and social revolutions we are facing have thrown our children into a world of confusion that we ourselves have not had to face. The questions running through their minds are forcing them to deal with issues at younger ages and earlier stages of development than ever before.[1]

Topics that had been settled years ago as facts (such as marriage and gender), never questioned by past generations, are now up for public debate and re-definition for our Generation Alpha children, who are too young to know how to critically assess these issues or deal with the fallout.

While there is nothing new under the sun—sin and evil have been prominent since the Garden of Eden—many aspects of modern culture definitely seem to be in a downward spiral. Our children have seen and experienced the serious erosion of the nuclear family, the redefining of marriage, and now gender. Principles which have traditionally been the stabilizing support for children are now creating increased problems rather than helping to alleviate them. Cohabitation before marriage, divorce, absent fathers, and single parent households are now common place.[2]

Most statistics tell us that approximately half of all marriages today will end in divorce.[3]

Married couples are now in the minority. Children are more likely to live in single-parent households — and in greater numbers than any age group before them. Historically, kids in single-parent households have been more likely to struggle compared to their peers in two-parent families. For instance, kids raised by just one parent run a higher risk of dropping out of school, experiencing an early pregnancy, and divorcing their spouse in adulthood.[4] Judeo-Christian ethics are being increasingly eroded with each generation.

Our culture has warped God's design for sexuality.

The beauty, love, and commitment that God intended to be fundamental to the gift of sex within marriage between a husband and wife have been distorted beyond recognition. Pornography is now at epidemic levels. The result is not satisfaction and fulfillment but loneliness, pain, and confusion, leaving a whole generation desperate for true intimacy.

Gender confusion is trendy.

The world is sending our children unbiblical messages of gender fluidity resulting in issues related to gender identities, gender roles, same-sex attraction, and sexual fulfillment. One day at school, "Michael" is in the cafeteria line and the next day, it's "Mary." Jane and Julie walk around hand-in-hand, and Steve wears a "dress."

I can't imagine the questions that swirl around in the minds of our children.

Can you imagine the confusion that must enter a child's mind when they realize that they have two moms or even more bewilderingly, two dads? Sixty-three percent of LGBTQ Millennials (aged 18-35) are considering expanding their families, either by becoming parents for the first time or by having more children by using assisted reproductive technology, foster care, or adoption.[5] This introduces a whole new complication to the discussion. Each of these issues will have a significant effect on the emotional and behavioral development of our children. Is it any wonder these kids are confused?

Terms have been redefined. "Diversity" and "inclusivity" used to define differing social and ethnic backgrounds, but now they signal the rejection of a person. Gender Dysphoria used to be a clinically significant diagnosed mental issue but has now become a "feeling of discomfort" related to a preference.

As if this weren't enough, the larger picture is a further reflection of how dark our world has become: worldwide pandemics, ongoing wars, mass shootings in cities and schools that they attend.

> Kids today are exposed to the constant media coverage of every shocking or immoral event. It all happens right in front of their eyes.

Are our children still safe outside? Can they walk across the street to play with their friends? Is that car following them? Can they eat a piece of candy without it needing to be screened for drugs?

Self-harm, suicide, abortion, sex trafficking, fentanyl overdoses are seemingly commonplace. Every news headline spews the sickening facts of the latest tragedy. Unspeakable!

Are you depressed yet? I am!

The world is going mad, and our kids have access and exposure to it all on the devices in their back pockets. With these cultural challenges at the forefront of our children's minds, we must address these challenges and prepare our kids for the onslaught of pressures they will inevitably face.

If we don't, who will? How many more children are we prepared to lose?

Indoctrination and a Secular Worldview

One issue that stands front and center of every question in our wonderful world is the current understanding of absolute truth. There is no such thing anymore. Relativism is rampant. The culture has shifted in the way in which it defines truth.

> Postmodernism says there is no absolute truth. Existentialism says that your "truth" might be different from my "truth". What is right for you is right and what is right for me is right. If it's OK for me, then it's good.

The introduction of situational ethics in the 1900's, along with the accompanying "flexibility" it necessitated, only worsened the situation. Situational ethics takes into account only the particular context of an action when assessing it ethically, rather than judging it according to any absolute moral standards.

One looks to an individual's ideals of what is appropriate to guide them, rather than an unchanging universal code of conduct. There is no right or wrong, no black and white, but rather, every situation is filtered through the lens of an individual's perspective of what they believe to be true and right.

The school systems, academia, and media have all adopted this approach. Even worse, in some cases, so has the church. This shift in culture has infiltrated the church with more than 50% of Christians now agreeing that there are no absolutes, and moral truth is up to the individual to decide.[6]

I'm OK. You're OK. If it feels good, do it. Truth is whatever you see it is. Faith is OK, if it works for you.

The Bible's stance on truth is in direct conflict with the society in which our kids are growing up.

Take a stand for biblical truth, and you are now labeled narrow-minded, intolerant, or worse, a bigot. Not a wonderful thing to be labeled as, especially since our underlying goal is to love everyone like Jesus loves.

> The mantra of relativism is tolerance, inclusiveness, and approval of all lifestyles and beliefs, even those which are in direct opposition to the Word of God.

With all of these going on in our culture, there is a very real race for the souls of our children. False religion, atheism, pantheism, secular humanism, and a host of other "isms" are racing to reach them.

We must be the first ones there.

Children now have access to more belief systems, more opinions and more voices than ever before. In the past, there may have been a few lone voices sending different messages, but for the most part, parents' voices could be strengthened by what a pastor and a few teachers were saying.

Now that has been reversed. Most of the voices screaming at children are the ones they are hearing through social media and the various kinds of online activity, and unfortunately, they often don't agree with what the parents and churches are communicating.

Valerie Bell, the author of a great book entitled *Resilient: Child Discipleship and the Fearless Future of the Church*, tells of a conversation that she had with two Awana missionaries from Africa:

> "Do you know what the Muslims are doing in Africa?" they asked me. "They are building mosques and schools with oil money from the Middle East. Any child can get a free education. He or she just has to attend the mosque and then they can attend school gratis . . . What poor parent, even Christian, can walk away from the offer of free education for their children? That is how they are recruiting for the future. They are starting very young, with small children."[7]

Does that sound familiar at all?

We are seeing that similar cultural reinforcement of a secular worldview here in the United States. Humanism and postmodernism engulf our children through the TV, school, celebrities, friends, social media, political messaging and more.

Even amongst professing Christians, 61 percent agree with

ideas rooted in new spirituality; 54 percent resonate with post-modernist views; 36 percent accept ideas associated with Marxism; and 29 percent believe ideas based on secularism.[8]

The outlook is not positive.

The days of valuing the messages from parents, teachers, and pastors have been replaced by the competing voices of social media and online activity. And at the younger ages, kids cannot differentiate between these different voices. "They don't have the objectivity to judge which voices are worth listening to and which are not."[9]

Our entire culture is aggressively indoctrinating our children with their secular worldview, and in churches, we are teaching wonderful Bible stories without connecting the stories to the real world.

No wonder we are losing these kids.

The Impact of COVID-19

To further complicate this "wonderful world" in which we live is the recent exposure to the worldwide pandemic, an event which has changed us all.

> Experts tell us that the age at which we're exposed to a traumatic event determines the depth of its manifestation in our soul.

In other words, children and teens who are in their formative years are more likely to be impacted and feel more anxious, overwhelmed, and unprepared than any other generation as a result of the time we spent responding to this virus.

Generation Z likely felt the impact most.

They were the ones most affected when their significant life events disappeared from their calendars during the various lockdowns.

- Schools and universities closed and remote education became the norm.
- School formals and graduations were cancelled and gap years were delayed.
- Sports schedules emptied and vacations were spent at home.
- Social lives almost ceased to exist.

One of the biggest impacts of COVID-19 was on people's health—not just their physical health but their mental health, wellbeing, and resilience.

Our children and teens are now suffering from a skyrocketing number of mental health issues. Complaints of boredom, depression, loneliness, and anxiety are rife amongst teenagers. Gen Z is now known as the most anxious generation ever, suffering from an expanding variety of mental health problems, more than any other generation of kids in American history.

- In the fall of 2020, it was estimated that one in four young adults contemplated suicide in the last month and similar numbers exist for those who meet the criteria for having a serious mental illness.[10]
- A study published in the summer of 2022 by researchers at Boston University shows that over 60 percent of college students met the criteria for mental

illness between 2020 and 2021 (during the coronavirus pandemic), which represents twice the rate from 2013.

- Depression and anxiety are up 135 percent and 110 percent respectively, and the rates of eating disorders increased by 96 percent. Non-suicidal self-injury increased by almost 46 percent, and suicidal ideation by 64 percent.[11]
- Forty-four percent of teenagers felt hopeless or persistently sad in the first few months of 2021 and 55 percent said they experienced emotional abuse at home.[12]

Why the increase in mental health conditions?

Is it personality? Home and family situations? Personal trauma? The rapid pace of change? Perhaps even a greater awareness of mental health conditions?

We are now raising the most medicated generation of kids in modern history. Diagnoses of anxiety disorders, ADHD, panic attacks, OCD, PTSD, bipolar disorders, eating disorders, psychoses, allergies, and other phobias are now commonplace among the American population.

While many legitimately need medication to control their situation, could it be possible that with some, this is a quick fix solution? A first resort rather than a last one? A band aid concealing a bigger problem? A way to avoid the need to build healthy coping skills? A substitute for a stable family life? A shortcut to self-discipline?

Experts agree that COVID-19 will also be a "defining moment" for our youngest children, known now as Generation Alpha.

Parents and teachers are often frustrated with their seeming addiction to their devices, yet when the pandemic forced schools to close and most workers to operate remotely, what was the solution?

Technology!

Screen time skyrocketed as the screens themselves became their classrooms and substitute childcare.

Families were confined to their homes.

Kids were unable to visit friends, play in the park, or visit their grandparents.

So, what did they do? They turned to their screen.

It may be years before we fully grasp the extent to which this major global event will impact this generation.

Interestingly, the Centers for Disease Control and Prevention (CDC) points to what they consider to be a possible solution to this devastating impact.

> The COVID-19 pandemic has created traumatic stressors that have the potential to further erode students' mental well-being. Our research shows that surrounding youth with the proper support can reverse these trends and help our youth now and in the future.[13]

Read that again!

"Our research shows that surrounding youth with **the proper support** can reverse these trends."

CDC's answer is "relationships." And they are right.

We must work more diligently to form meaningful relationships with our kids.
We must love them at the deepest level of their needs.
We must answer their cry for help with a caring friend.
We must support them as they confront the issues of our ever-darkening world.

We must also engage with the issues our kids are facing. Unfortunately, most churches live in a bubble of niceties, smiling and shaking hands in a superficial way, while people smile back through their tears. Their pain and trauma are kept at a comfortable distance as we focus on our programs and protocols.

We spend our time teaching wonderful Bible stories, neither addressing the hurt nor discussing the solutions. Please don't get me wrong, Bible "stories" are great, and we obviously need good Bible teaching. But we must also address the issues outside the walls of the safety of the church.

We are losing kids and their families at an alarming rate. We must ask ourselves, "Why are they leaving?"

Louis Armstrong's wonderful world has become a dark and dangerous playground, and we need to call our children to come inside.

We need to address the reasons why families are leaving the church in droves.

We must explore the reasons why teens and young adults are saying that the church is irrelevant.

We need to understand why they are saying that they no longer believe.

We must answer the accusations that are being made against the church and begin to restore trust.

We cannot continue to allow the distractions to steal the future of our children.

We must do whatever it takes to get their attention.

Don't leave them outside.

The world is getting darker and it's not safe.

Call them in!

It's time to come in!

3

A Moving Target: Different Kids, Different Needs

It's easy to think and write about the many needs in children's ministry while I'm sitting here by the pool in the warm ocean breeze overlooking the beach. But I understand the reality of kid's ministry is so much harder. The busy life of a children's ministry leader leaves little time to stop and think, let alone read a book about change.

We are so encumbered by the seemingly endless administrative tasks that to stop and evaluate major changes is just not on our "to-do list". The urgent takes precedence over the important.

But we know the statistics and it's not good news. Seventy-five percent of kids who are raised in the church are leaving when they grow into adulthood and no longer have their parents nagging them to attend on Sundays.

We've known that for a while.

What we might not know is that the age of their departure is becoming younger. Kids are now leaving the church as they enter middle school, and their parents are leaving with them.[14]

We can see the empty chairs of the missing children.

Perhaps it was baseball season, with its multiple regular weekly practices which placed a time crunch on a family you know, only they didn't return when the season ended.

Maybe it was the quarterly dance recital with its accelerated rehearsal schedule, which they told you was "only temporary," but their return attendance was sporadic and then non-existent.

Thankfully, some new families came, and they filled the missing gaps and even perhaps reduced the urgency of finding out why the others were gone. But what about the others? What happened to them? Why did they leave? We ask ourselves, "Could I have done something to prevent it? Is there something I can do to draw them back?"

Is there any hope, or are we resigned to losing more and more children, perhaps even an entire generation?

Valerie Bell is extremely insightful on this topic. She writes:

> Today's church kids are growing up in both a secular and church culture that are unlike the cultures in which most adults grew up . . . I fear our assumptions of "sameness"—our cluelessness in the midst of huge cultural shifts—may lead us to be unresponsive to the needs these shifts present.[15]

With more resources than we've ever had, it still seems that the kids are more spiritually distant than ever before. How can this be? It's not that we aren't trying. We work from dawn to dusk to be creative and relevant.

But with a retention rate of only one in four kids staying in the church, we need to ask ourselves some tough questions.

Where have we gone wrong?

Why are so many leaving the church?

The target has moved, but have we adjusted our radar? Are we meeting the needs of this new culture? Are we guilty of assuming "sameness" in our ministry?

My husband grew up hunting and wanted me to learn to, at least be able to handle a gun safely. We spent some time doing target practice, and I have to say, I was pretty good for an amateur. At least that's what I thought, until he had me try trap shooting. In trap shooting, you load a round clay target into a machine, which then flings the clay target into the air. The flying clay is intended to simulate the action of a live target. When I tried this, I didn't hit a single target. Turns out shooting is a completely different task when the target is moving.

In the same way, our kid's ministry target is different than it was. The children of this generation have so many different needs and life challenges than in the past, and my guess is that most of our ministries consist of the same old approach.

> The challenge for the Church is that our current children's ministry systems were designed for a different era . . . Gen Z and now Gen Alpha need a different system.[16]

When was the last time you reassessed your target? Have you adjusted your sight? Can you perceive the shift?

We must understand our audience well enough to know how to reach them.

> The church in America risks losing more families if we are not willing to rethink our approach to children's ministry.

We must stop the hemorrhaging of the children and families who are leaving in droves for what may appear to be greener pastures, but in fact, is an ever-darkening world. George Barna, the founder of the Barna Group, a market research firm specializing in studying the religious beliefs and behavior of Americans, says that "it will require unprecedented imagination and collaboration in approaches to children's ministry."[17]

"Unprecedented imagination and collaboration."

I know—you don't have time to do that. It's difficult enough to keep up with the week-to-week planning and processing of your ministry. Well, that is the purpose of *When you see Fireflies*. Don't give up. Our target might be moving, but we have the answers. Don't be discouraged. There is hope! Please keep reading.

Forgetting what is behind and straining toward what is ahead, I press on toward the goal . . . (Phil. 3:13-14 NIV)

PART TWO

HEAR: Check the Time

There are about 2,000 known firefly species, and about 125 of these species reside in North America, mostly in the southeastern United States. They are known by a wide variety of names including lightning bugs, forest stars, glow flies, golden sparklers, fire devils, candle flies, moon bugs, big dippers, blinkies, and flying embers.

This generation of children to whom we are privileged to work with are as unique as the firefly. Never before has a generation been born into a world of technology. Previous generations have been introduced gradually. Not so with these children.

They will never know a world without cell phones, iPads, and the internet.

They will never know what it's like to use a pay phone.

They will never send a telegram.

They will always be surrounded by the pressures of social media.

They are unique!

We must learn to understand them if we hope to reach them.

What are their unique characteristics and needs?

We need to listen to their questions and provide answers.

We need to hear them!

Check the time before it's too late!

4

Legal Resident Aliens: Who is Generation Alpha?

When I moved from my home in Australia to America, I came on a student visa. I spent the next eighteen months completing my Master of Theology degree, and during that time I met my husband. Once I graduated, we were married and I needed to change my legal status in order to be able to remain in the country. I received a "Green Card" and became a "Legal Resident Alien."

Seriously!

That is what was written across the top of a card that is actually not green! I was considered a foreigner in my new adopted home.

I was in fact different, and sometimes, people wondered about my words and actions. While I looked the same as Americans, I spoke a different "language," had many cultural idiosyncrasies, and often had a different perspective. I was in some senses, an "alien".

It's the same way with the kids we work with today. They often seem like aliens, flown into our world by a foreign stork. They speak a foreign language with all of their slang, abbreviations, and jargon. Sometimes, their behavior also leaves us wondering.

> Youth today love luxury. They have bad manners, contempt for authority, no respect for older people and talk nonsense when they should be working. They contradict their parents, talk too much in company, guzzle their food, lay their legs on the table and tyrannize their elders.

This quote could certainly be the sentiment of someone describing today's children. But in actuality, it's attributed to Socrates, the classical Greek philosopher who lived around 470–399 BC, complaining about the youth of Athens. It's difficult to imagine that nearly two thousand years later, the kids sound the same.

Young people often receive a bad rap from the older generations for their bad behavior, but negative stereotyping and generalizing do nothing to improve the situation. Compassion and understanding will produce more positive results than assumptions.

Some will view this new generation as device addicted, overindulged, and unreliable.

Those who are discerning might have a different perspective, instead of seeing them as resilient, digitally savvy, more creative, and confident.

Perhaps they are a bit of both.

Yes, they are different, and they can be frustrating. But if we are going to connect with them on a deeper level, we must seek to truly understand them and their unique needs. Loving instruction will always accomplish more than judgment and assumptions.

Different Kids, Different Needs

The children we are working with now are very different from their Generation Z and millennial predecessors.

Generation Z are the teens and young adults (ages 12-26), the last of whom are aging out of kid's ministry. The millennial generation, aged between 27-42 years, are the parents of the children in our ministries.

The children that we are working with are the next generation—Generation Alpha.

A social research analyst from Australia was working on a book about the emerging and yet unnamed generation. He conducted a survey to find out what people thought the generation after Z should be called. Generation A was the most common suggestion, but he was not a fan. Instead, he looked to the model of hurricane names where the names ran through the usual Roman or Latin alphabet and then on to the Greek alphabet. He settled on the next cohort being Generation Alpha—not a return to the old, but the start of something new."[18]

Born between 2010 and 2025, this new generation labeled "Generation Alpha" (the first generation to be born only within the 21st century), is an entirely different entity. At the time of writing, the oldest in this generation are 12 year olds, while the youngest are yet to be born.

Each generational cycle lasts approximately 15 years.

Table 1: Timeline of twentieth century generations

Generations	Timeline
GIs	1901–1924
Silents	1925–1945
Baby Boomers	1946–1964
Baby Busters/Generation X	1965–1980
Millennials/Generation Y	1981–1996
iGens/Generation Z	1997–2010
Generation Alpha	2010–2025

Generation Alpha are considered by their millennial parents to be a precious gift in a time of extreme difficulty.

Do you know these kids?

Do you understand them?

Have you made appropriate adjustments for them, or are we just assuming that "kids are kids"?

Why do we need to understand them?

If we can't understand, communicate with, and connect with Alphas, we will be irrelevant.

One of the key characteristics of a leader is foresight—being able to see things as they will become. As leaders, we must be aware and ready for this change. We must understand Alphas!

Generation Alpha are predicted to become the largest generation in the history of the world, totaling almost two billion globally by 2025. While the characteristics of each generation don't usually begin to appear until they are older, a picture of Generation Alpha is starting to emerge.

They Will Be More Educated

Analysts believe that Alphas will grow up to be the best-educated generation ever. Compared to prior generations, they will be more likely to earn a college degree and more likely to be surrounded by college-educated adults.[19]

They are likely to stay in their education environment longer, begin their earning years later, and consequently, live at home with their parents longer than their predecessors. They will move more frequently, change careers more often, and increasingly live in urban, not just suburban, environments.[20]

They Will Have Increased Wealth

Alphas will also be surrounded by more wealth. Half of Americans (48%) now say that two is the ideal number of children for a family to have, reflecting a decades-long preference for a smaller family over a larger one.[21]

> Subsequently, their Alpha children are the most pampered and wealthiest in terms of materialistic possessions and gadgets, making them an instant gratification seeker, selfish and overindulged cohort.[22]

They Will Reflect Increased Racial Diversity

Generation Alpha is also on track to become the nation's most racially and ethnically diverse generation thus far.

Between 2000 and 2010, the Hispanic population grew by 43 percent, accounting for more than half of the increase in the total U.S. population.

The Asian population grew faster than any other major race group.[23]

The bottom line: Alphas will consist of a high number of children with foreign-born parents and children who are foreign-born themselves, representing more countries around the world than previous generations. Census population projections estimate that white America will be in the minority by 2045.

They Will Have a Greater Global Influence

The world is fully accessible to Generation Alpha, thanks to technology. Their devices allow them to be more aware of current trends, movies, music, celebrities, and influencers, each enabling a reach far wider than in the previous generations.

Fashion, food, online entertainment, social trends, communication, viral YouTube videos, and memes are all part of Alpha's "education."

They Will Have a More Mobile Lifestyle

This generation is also predicted to be more mobile in many areas of their life, including where, when, and how they will work, study, travel, and live.

Tele-work, flexi-time, work from home or remote working, working in shifts, and rise in dual-career families have already blurred the boundaries between personal and professional life for the parents, which no doubt will impact their Alpha children.

Today, the average length of staying in one working role has shortened to just under three years, which means Alphas could possibly have up to 18 different jobs over the course of their life.

Encouraging the Future: How do we do it?

Yes, they are still a bit of a mystery to us.

The first step to connecting with Gen Alpha is to realize that they are already here. They are the kids in your children's ministry. They are a new generation, and they speak a different language.

We have not yet touched on the greatest difference—their engagement with technology. For many of us who belong to the Boomer or the Buster generations, technology is an entirely foreign language, yet this is how they communicate. They were born into it and it's naive to think that we can remove it from their world.

Like it or not, technology is here to stay, and we must accept that. Once we do, we can begin to think of ways to integrate it into their world in a positive and productive way.

How do we do that?

Keep reading.

5

Addicts or Experts? Technology is Their Second Language

Technology! An addiction or an expertise?

The year 2010 was the first year of this new generation, and, ironically, was the year that iPads were launched, Instagram was created, and "app" was the American Dialect Society's word of the year.

Generation Alpha was quite literally born into a world of technology.

Our assessment of this generation's interaction with technology can be summarized in two different ways:

Technology is an addiction; a habit that must be broken.

OR . . .

Technology is a doorway for future innovators and experts.

Whichever perspective we hold, we must understand and accept that technology is now a second language to the newer generations. It's not going away, nor can we remove it.

Alphas have a relationship with technology unlike any other previous generations.

While Generation Z probably didn't receive their first digital screens until their later school years, and the purpose of those screens was likely educational, for Generation Alpha, technology has been present from the beginning. Gen Alpha will never know a world without devices. Their identities are being shaped by social media. It is who they are. It is everywhere!

While squirming at a restaurant, Dad shoved a phone into their little hands to enable adult conversation.

When grandma babysat, she became tired and handed them iPad so they could watch a movie.

To make dinner preparation possible, Mom downloaded the latest game onto her laptop and allowed her preschooler to play.

For Generation Alpha, their toys are smartphones and iPads.[24]

By the age of two, they are able to master touchscreens and easily navigate through various apps on smartphones . . . earning them the labels of *screenagers*, *digital natives*, and *connected* or *wired generation.*[25] They have become known as "Generation Glass" because of their numerous devices.

Alphas learn by doing, and they are not afraid of devices. They readily experiment, touching buttons and exploring drop-down menus to learn what will happen. They know that most actions are reversible, so they click, and explore, and more importantly, learn.

Did you know that more than half (65%) of children ages 8 to 11 already own or have access to a mobile phone?[26] Eight-year-old children walk around today with the world in the palm of their hands or in their back pockets.

It is estimated that kids ages 8-12 spend 6-8 hours a day on their devices.

> Worn on their wrist, in their back pockets, all day in school, they use it to work, shop, learn, connect and play, because the glass that they interact on now and will wear on their wrist, as glasses on their face, that will be on the Head Up Display of the driverless car they are transported in, or the interactive school desk where they learn will transform how they work, shop, learn, connect and play.[27]

Often while we are hanging out, our youngest daughter will often refer to the latest trend, fashion, video, or song. I often wonder how she learned about so many things that never touched my world. Her answer? YouTube or Tik Tok, the latest and greatest sources of information for our children.

Consider "artificial intelligence" (otherwise known as the familiar voices of Siri, Alexa, and Google Assistant).

Our kids know them well, and in fact connect with them more than they do with their parents or friends.

"Alexa, remind me to call Sara."

"Hey Siri—where is the closest Thai restaurant?"

"Hey Siri—What is the latest trend?"

"Hey Siri—what is fentanyl?"

It's scary that these kids have the ability to learn on the internet, and the information is so accessible AND ANONYMOUS! No one knows that they asked.

Experts are telling us that there are downsides to the increased technology access and connectivity.

- They are seeing effects on cognitive development, from the premature thinning in the brain's cortex to neuronal changes[28] and shorter attention spans.[29]

- Psychological and mental health issues have increased, along with delayed social development.
- There are physiological concerns with sleep deprivation[30] and a lack of exercise[31] with the prolonged sitting while staring at devices.
- Children are losing their sense of wonder and innocence as they are exposed to information which they may not be ready to handle emotionally.
- Safety and cyber security issues have led to increased cyberbullying, easier access for sex predators and traffickers, along with increased exposure to pornography.

Convinced yet? Technology is everywhere, and our kids are immersed in it. The statistics are overwhelming and make me want to destroy every device I see.

I recently volunteered at a summer camp and was shocked to see several of the 8-year-olds in my group carrying their own iPhone. They were only eight! Why does an 8-year-old need a phone? They were quite proud of their personal device and waved it in front of the others in the group. I felt like grabbing it and tossing it in the trash can, but I can also acknowledge that this is an unhelpful reaction.

> However, it is naive to think that we can remove technology from their lives. Technology is here to stay, and we must learn how to deal with it.

Viewed from the other perspective, this birth into technology is developing a generation of expertise that has never existed before.

A survey conducted to 8,000 parents of Alpha children across the world revealed that eight is the age parents think their kids' knowledge of technology outstrips their own.[32]

Might this exposure to technology have a good side? We will have to wait and see, but it's certain that this generation will take us to places that we have never been before. Robotics, artificial intelligence, coding, app development, and data analytics will have new developments that will no doubt transform our world beyond our imagination.

Are these kids addicts or experts, or even both?

How should we respond?

While Alphas might have nearly unlimited access to information, they still need adults to help them translate that knowledge into wisdom. They need adults to direct them to the reputable sources of material. They need us to guide them safely.

There will be technology no matter what, so the question is whether we will be there to guide the context of how children interpret what they are experiencing.

Can we help our kids discover God by using the range of available technology?

Can we adjust our teaching to incorporate these new innovations?

Is there a way to use technology for good?

6

Tigers or Helicopters? A Parents' Fearful Response

Confronted with this new generation of uniqueness, parents are struggling to know how to deal with their kids. Confusion and fear are overwhelming them, and parents are asking for help. Parenting has become much more complicated with today's tensions.

Do we allow children independence versus keeping them safe?

Do we expose them to the real world versus sheltering them?

Balancing issues like these are difficult at the best of times.

First, let's look at the parents.

Children today are being raised by parents who are millennials (1981-1996). They are diverse, highly educated, and most of them are digital experts. They were raised during the era of the Clinton scandal, O.J. Simpson trial, 9/11, Princess Diana, the Columbine shooting, the 2008 housing crisis, recessions, the war in the Middle East, Y2K, and the birth of the internet.

They began their parenting experience with a rich and unique set of experiences in life and career. They also have a mistrust of institutions, and perhaps have experienced their own turbulent journey of doubts about Christianity or the church.[33]

They tend to be older than parents were in the past, choosing to begin their families once their careers are established. Education is now more readily accessible and results in a later entrance to the workforce, often delaying the moving out of home.[34] The average age of first-time parents is now in the early thirties.[35]

While confident in other aspects of their lives, fear reigns supreme when it comes to parenting. Can you blame them? Every day, the 24/7 news cycle broadcasts stories of terror, school shootings, drug and alcohol abuse, cyber-bullying, abductions, and human trafficking.[36] These devasting issues saturate our country to a seemingly immeasurable and irreversible degree.

Anxiety, depression, self-destructive behavior, crime, suicide, sex trafficking, child abuse, abortion, homelessness, gender identity issues and sexuality, self-esteem and body image, cancel culture, peer influence, digital content, video games, social media, family struggles . . .

These are just the short list of issues plaguing our world today.

The fear is understandable and palpable. Parents are afraid for their children, and they are most commonly responding in one of two extremes. They are becoming "tigers" or "helicopters".

Tiger Parenting

Tiger parents are fearful of failure, so they are obsessed and consumed with doing whatever it takes to ensure the future success of their children.

"Tiger Parents" drive the academic and social successes of their children through an authoritarian approach.

Tiger parents register their children in early learning programs, sign them up for extra practices, and fill their days with a never-ending list of activities, all designed to stay ahead of the crowd.

Tiger parents enroll their children in top-performing schools and pay for after-school tuition to ensure their kids are given every opportunity to get high grades. Ultimately, they hope this will then lead to acceptance into a high-ranking university and a prestigious future profession.[37]

Tiger parents schedule multiple after-school activities for their children to help them get ahead: piano classes, dance lessons, back-to-back sports, keeping their schedules full year-round.

Tiger parents hope for an athletic scholarship for their child and are willing to use vacation time to attend sports tournaments. The competitive youth sports have become a $15 billion dollar industry,[38] increasing by 55 percent since 2010.[39] Parents are spending more than ten percent of their annual household income on registration fees, travel, camps and equipment.[40] And you better believe it. Tiger parents are the ones driving the industry.

Because their kids are their "trophies" and a reflection of how well they teach and raise them, they (parents, teachers, coaches, and leaders) have become focused on the fear that their children won't be safe, won't be happy, and won't reach their potential.[41]

Will they be accepted into the best schools?

Will they get a scholarship?

Will they marry a respectable person?

Will they find a decent job and earn enough money?

Social media increases the pressure to compete when fellow parents post their latest success, their recent perfect vacation, or their child's latest achievements. Parents read these posts and desire the same for their family, conceding their otherwise valued standards for the sake of their child's happiness, or worse, keeping up with the Joneses.

The result of tiger parenting is an all-consuming busyness. Sports used to involve one practice a week and one game. Now, it is usually multiple sessions each week. Dance classes used to be for enjoyment, but now we have regular public recitals which require increased rehearsals, expensive leotards, and costumes. Piano lessons, school theatre, and homework have to fit somewhere in the midst of the hectic schedule.

But in reality, tiger parents are chasing their tail.

The truth is that only two percent of high school athletes go on to play for a NCAA Division 1 school[42] and very few will ever grace the doorstep of The Juilliard School of Performing Arts.

The real reason for driving their children and holding a whip in front of them is fear.

Parents are afraid.

They desire the best for their children and are ferociously protecting them from failure at all costs in the best way they know how.

The resulting hectic schedule has squeezed the family so tightly that church attendance and faith have been shifted to the edge. The avenue which can bring balance and peace is the one which has been forced to the bottom rung of the priority ladder.

What hope, then, do these parents have if they have no time for God?

Helicopter Parenting

The contrasting response to this fear is known as 'helicopter' parenting.

> Helicopter parents are driven by the desperate desire for their child's safety and protection.

Helicopter parents hover and pay extremely close attention to their kids' activities and schoolwork to protect them from all pain and disappointment.

Helicopter parents will advocate for their misbehaving children rather than allowing the punishment. They will confront their teachers and coaches for correcting or talking harshly to their children.

Helicopter parents are even known to do the homework for their kids.

Helicopter parents cushion their children from the inevitable consequences of life instead of allowing them to build determination, resolve, and strength.

These parents worry about their kids wandering free in parks or on the streets with friends, because society is perceived as not being as safe for kids as it once was. Every abduction story, outbreak, allergy, injury, and statistic we read about can lead us to become uncertain as to whether we're doing everything we can to guarantee our child's growth, health, and well-being.

We are hovering, and society has only added to our actions.

In 2013, concerns about injuries at a middle school led to a ban during recess where kids could no longer play with footballs, baseballs, soccer balls, or anything else that might hurt someone on school grounds.[43] School administrators replaced the athletic equipment with soft Nerf balls, and playing tag and doing cartwheels without a coach were banned. The school's superintendent explained that there had been an excess of injuries that warranted this policy. After all, experts say that without helmets and pads, kids can get hurt. Students were understandably upset since they spent their whole day sitting behind a desk learning, but parental concern and lawsuits overruled their objections.

Parents (and society) are going to extreme lengths in an effort to smooth out the hardships which might confront their children. This pattern of parenting appears to be polarized with excessive love, affection, and continuous monitoring.[44] Unfortunately, this overprotectiveness can backfire. If we try to remove every obstacle and solve every problem, our children will never learn to handle the pain and trouble, which they will inevitably face in life.

> The truth is that kids are naturally fearless and anti-fragile. We actually contribute to their fragility with our hovering and overprotectiveness.

Have you ever watched a toddler learn to walk? I remember the day when our first child began to walk. She toddled a few steps, fell, and then laughed hysterically. I guess she found it funny. But she repeated that over and over, walking a little farther each time, before falling down and laughing.

Toddlers fall and get up, and fall and get up again. They bump their heads, their elbows, and their knees. But they just keep going. Why? They are determined to reach their toy or move independently where their interest takes them. "I can do it myself" is their mantra.

We are the ones that instill their fear.

Watch a young child a few years older. Now when they fall, the child has learned to look to the adults nearby to seek out their response. If adults panic and quickly rush to the child, the child is conditioned to panic as well. They mirror our emotions.[45]

Our reaction instills fear and instead of responding with resilience, they cry and raise their arms. We instantly pick them, wipe their tears, and sooth their panic.

Deep down, parents know that fear is not a good motivator.

They don't know what else to do but react.

They are asking for help in the enormous task of parenting, and they often look to the church for support, encouragement, and answers.

What should our response be?

7

Return to the Blueprint: A Family Ministry Mandate

Any set of parents who attends church on a regular basis likely already knows that as parents, they are the ones who are responsible for their children's spiritual development. The Bible makes it crystal clear that it is the role and responsibility of the parents (literally the father) to raise their children in the nurture and admonition of the Lord (Eph. 6:4). Most parents already understand this concept.

The Old Testament is clear that it is incumbent, primarily upon the father of a family, to impart instruction to his young children. Moses reminds the Israelites to pass their early memories of the Exodus along to their children and retell the stories often.

> *Do not forget the things your eyes have seen or let them fade from your heart as long as you live. Teach them to your children and to their children after them.* (Deut. 4:9)[46]

Time and again, it's made clear that fathers are to teach their children, and furthermore, to their children's children (grandchildren).

> *And these words which I command you today shall be in your heart. You shall teach them diligently to your children, and shall talk of them when you sit in your house, when you walk by the way, when you lie down, and when you rise up. You shall bind them as a sign on your hand, and they shall be as frontlets between your eyes. You shall write them on the doorposts of your house and on your gates.* (Deut. 6:6-9)[47]

This section of the Old Testament is known as the Shema, the central statement of the Jewish faith. It is as familiar today to Jewish people as John 3:16 is to Christians. It teaches parents that they are to be "diligent" about forming the character of their children, using every teachable opportunity possible to share God's Word with them.

The passage says to "Teach . . . *diligently.*" This is the translation of a Hebrew word that has the meaning of "repeat" or "say again and again." The "teaching" is meant to be reinforced by the words, "*shall talk of them.*" Other translations say, "Recite them . . . and talk about them," "repeat them . . . and speak of them," "tell them . . . and keep on telling them."[48]

This "teaching" would include planned times of talking (e.g., mealtimes), impromptu times (e.g., walking, driving), bedtime (reflection at the end of the day), and mornings (preparing for a new day). They were to wear the instructions on their hands and bodies (like wearing a cross or a bracelet), and post it on the doorposts of their homes (the last thing you see when leaving and first when arriving) as a visible testimony to neighbors.

The entire family living in a tent together in Old Testament times would certainly have made those interactions more convenient than our overscheduled lives today, but regardless, the command still stands.

It is a profound responsibility, but sadly, research seems to indicate that this is most often missing, even in the more committed families. As a result, we are missing out on the spiritual heritage of previous generations, when we should be standing on the shoulders of our forefathers and learning from their wisdom. The results of this lack of instruction are as disastrous now as they were back then.

> *When all that generation had been gathered to their fathers, another generation arose after them who did not know the Lord nor the work which He had done for Israel.* (Judg. 2:10)

Each generation is needing to reinvent their faith when they ought to be building a bridge from the past to the present.

Moses finished his instruction to Israel, just as he began, making it clear that parents should be aware of their primary duty to obey God's word and teach it to future generations.

> *Moses finished speaking all these words to all Israel, and he said to them:*
>
> *'Set your hearts on all the words which I testify among you today, which you shall command your children to be careful to observe—all the words of this law'.* (Deut. 32:45-46)[49]

Instruction continues regularly throughout the rest of the Bible, teaching the need for parents to pray for their children,[50] and exhorting them to teach[51] and discipline them,[52] beginning when they are young.[53]

When it comes to the church, the question remains: what should our responsibility be?

> Interestingly, Scripture did not tell parents to bring their children to the temple or tabernacle (or to the church). It was the family's responsibility to teach their children.

Homes were and still are the perfect place to take advantage of those teachable moments.

Parents are the perfect people to do so, as no one knows and loves a child like a parent.

And while churches should be a valuable partner, the primary responsibility remains with the parents. It is the parents who will be held primarily accountable for the spiritual growth of their children, not the church.

Despite this responsibility, many Christian families confess their own struggles, operating from depleted faith resources as well as feelings of inadequacy or struggles fulfilling their own biblical calling. The complexities of life are enough to destroy the confidence of the most educated and trained professionals.

A study done by Lawrence, who was completing research for her dissertation on "Forming Faith in Families," found that 66 percent of committed Christian parents readily acknowledged the many challenges involved in nurturing the faith of their children.[54] Many adults admitted to struggling with their own spiritual inconsistences and being consistent with their Bible study and daily walk with the Lord.

Parents reported the difficulty they face in making time for intentional family devotions and spiritual activities. While it is their desire to help their children grow stronger in their own relationships with the Lord, they struggle to find the time to do so.[55]

Parents have willingly abdicated their discipleship responsibilities to the church. It's easy for parents to relinquish their responsibility, and it's been easy for the church to assume it. Denise Muirkjesbo of the Barna Group states it well:

> I fear that leaders in the church have inadvertently sent parents the message that the church is the primary keeper of the spiritual formation of children. We [send this message] with our well-trained leaders, amazing environments, powerful curriculum and life-changing (sometimes flashy) events. The message that many parents receive is, "This is what it takes to foster spiritual formation in children." Sadly, parents, grandparents, guardians and "faith friends" feel like they cannot compete with that or replicate what happens at church. So, they step back and defer to the church as the primary provider of spiritual formation of children.[56]

Parents are happy because their children are receiving some Bible teaching; the kids are happy because the churches are providing another source of entertainment; and the church is happy because it is serving people.

> "This sounds like a wonderful win-win situation except for one issue: *The approach is completely unbiblical!*"[57]

While the church is neither equipped nor called to circumvent the parents' God-given call to disciple their children, it is the church's responsibility to encourage and train them.

> We need to equip parents and teach them how to restore their influence in the lives of their children.

We can no longer assume that parents are engaged and involved in the lives of their kids.

We can no longer assume that parents are actively involved in their child's spiritual discipleship.

If the church had been successful at discipling parents, then kid's ministry would be helpful but not necessary. But because we have failed to disciple the adults, who should in turn be discipling their children, the formal kid's ministry in the church is necessary.[58]

This generation of children needs the church to step in.

Desperate parents who are frustrated and fearful, ill-equipped and unprepared, are all looking for help from a church that is also struggling, declining and evolving, and not always for the better.

We have definitely become more aware of this need to partner with parents, but research suggests that we are not doing well.[59]

We must remember that our children's ministry exists to partner with, to support, and to come alongside children's true faith-developers — the parents!

We need to find ways to encourage the parents and equip them for the task of biblical parenting in a world which is far from ideal.

The task lies with them, but we need to walk alongside them.

We need to assist them in this overwhelming responsibility.

We must return to the blueprint.

8

A New Happy Meal Toy: It's Time for a Change

Something needs to change.

We are losing families, and that is unacceptable.

Families are saying that the church is no longer relevant, or that they no longer believe.

Are you OK with losing a whole generation? I'm not. We must do something.

I can hear the objections already:

"What's wrong with what I'm doing?"

"I'm not changing! I don't have time to change."

"The Bible doesn't change so we shouldn't either."

I'm not suggesting that as children's ministry leaders we ever change our message. Jesus Christ is the same yesterday, today and forever, and His word is unchanging, but that doesn't mean we should be unchanging.

God's Word is timeless, and we should never compromise His message, but we must be willing to adjust the presentation of that message.
We must become more culturally relevant.
We must listen to what the new generations are saying.

Remember the kid's happy meals at McDonalds?

The food options are basically the same as they always have been:

Junior burger, small fries, and a small drink.

The item that constantly changes is the happy meal toy.

One month, it's a toy from the latest Minion movie.

The next month, it's 101 Dalmatians.

The meal remains constant, but the attraction adjusts to the latest trending cultural theme.

- Stay up on the latest TV channels, toys, movies, and apps.
- See what's trending on Netflix, Amazon, and Disney+ and check out the top kid's websites.
- Do a Google search to find out which kid's websites are visited most often.
- Check out which YouTube channels are the most popular with kids, and which books are best sellers for kids.

Visit their world every now and again to see the trends so you are able to relate more effectively.

While the biblical aspects of our children's ministry should always remain constant and the message uncompromised, we cannot assume that we are always being culturally applicable. The tactics that worked well in the past might not grab kid's attention today.

When asked why they don't prioritize church, the most common excuse is that many people feel their church has lost its relevance.

This is to be expected since it's a different time, a different culture, and these are different kids. It's time for a reexamination of our methodologies. Are you willing to change? Are you willing to go there? If so, keep reading!

They are Leaving

Where have the families gone?

So many have left the church and, worse, have abandoned their faith. Even if we think we are doing well, statistics tells us we're not. This has become obvious, notably because of the increased sporadic attendance.

Families that previously attended 3 out of 4 weeks now attend only twice a month.

Twice a month is considered the new "faithful."

Families that used to attend twice a month now attend just once a month or even less.

The category called the "churched adults" numbers approximately 124.4 million, and they are the ones who attend church at least once in a six-month period.[60] This is the group that we affectionately call the "CEOs," "Christmas and Easter Only".

Those who identify themselves as "practicing Christians," stating that they are "most committed" to their faith and that it is "very important" to them, also admit to attending church a minimum of only once a month.[61] Recent research shows that only 2 in 10 Americans under 30 years of age believe that attending a church is important or worthwhile (which is an all-time low).[62]

When families begin to habitually skip church for whatever reason, they are heading towards a slippery slope. They are sending a message to their children that church is not that important or a family priority. Other activities are given precedence, and church is just another option for how to spend a Sunday morning.

Jesus might be a part of our life, but He is not the center.

The Bible is a helpful book but not the greatest priority.

Parents whose own commitment is minimal are raising children who, not surprisingly, also possess a shallow, unnurtured faith. If their faith exists at all, it's likely that their convictions will crumble under the world's pressures that are sure to come their way.

When we were involved in church planting, we were working with new believers who were doing their best to replace their old lifestyle with new godly disciplines.

When it came to church attendance, the temptation to skip was great. If it was left to a decision each week, church, Bible study, or serving in a ministry usually lost out.

> The challenge for them was to move to a place where the issue of church attendance was already decided without discussion or question.

It wasn't a weekly decision; it was a given.

Their faith was the top priority, and that meant that church was non-negotiable.

Until families reach that level of maturity, church will always be only an option that will be circumvented when the temptation for something preferable comes along. Unfortunately, many families have not reached that place and their commitment to church wavers, depending on their weekly choices.

Let's help parents see the vital importance of making church a top priority.

Until we do, we shouldn't be surprised when we find that kids don't know basic Bible truths.

If they only attend church once every 3-4 weeks, how could they?

Many children who have parents who are separated or divorced, and live in a shared custody situation are often only able attend to church when they are with one of their parents. This translates to attending church every other week. They are missing 50-75 percent of the lessons. It really is no wonder they are biblically illiterate.

We must help parents understand that God doesn't want to just be a part of their life, but He wants to be the center of their life.

Church must be the priority, not just something to do if there is no sport going on or the weekend lake trip is rained out.

If God is not a priority for the parents, you can be sure that He won't be a priority for the children.

9

Our Task: Restoring Relevance, Trust, and Belief

Their issues for leaving are three-fold: families feel that church is no longer relevant, they have become disillusioned with the church, and, perhaps most tragically, they have abandoned their belief in God.

Restoring Relevance: Address the Hard Questions

The world is becoming darker by the day, and when unchurched people think about church, they often don't see a connection to their daily lives.

- One in four practicing Christian millennials believes that the church is irrelevant today (the same number as non-Christians).[63]
- Fifty-seven percent of churched adults and 45 percent of practicing Christians say they know people who are

tired of the same old church services; 40 percent of churched adults say they leave disappointed at least half the time.[64]

- Many of them say they are "tired" of church as they have known it growing up.
- Nearly three out of every four teens who have grown up in the church have quit going, and thousands more will join their ranks this week.[65]

The church is irrelevant?

"Irrelevant" is defined as "having no importance or relation to what is being considered," "being inapplicable or not pertinent; not connected with."[66]

Our entire culture is aggressively indoctrinating our children with their secular worldview, and our churches are perceived to be "irrelevant."

Churches continue to preach the good news, but is the church addressing the questions our kids are asking?

Are they right? Have we become irrelevant? How can that be?

> We have the truth, and we have the answers.
> We know who wins in the end, but are we communicating this to our families?
> Are we addressing the felt needs and questions of a new generation and its families?
> Are we failing to connect to the real world?

Church is for faith, not work, school, money, mental health, and a host of other real-world issues, right? People in our communities are asking questions, and they are not sure if the church is really answering them. The problems which we are dealing with have been around for centuries but are resurfacing in a different way with an unstoppable force, brought on by the onslaught of technology and social media. Are we speaking to those issues?

We need to provide biblical solutions to their felt needs.

If we leave them empty, why would they come?

The parents are fearful and feel overwhelmed.

They don't know what to do.

They want our help.

If we were responding effectively, would we be losing so many?

We have to answer the difficult questions. How is the church addressing these issues? How should the church speak to these issues?

Let's use the issue of morality as an example.

Forty to fifty percent of high schoolers now admit to being sexually active.[67]

Parents are deeply concerned and rightly so.

The world has distorted sex, separating it from the love and commitment of God's intended design. With tragic regularity, the internet and social media promote the enticements and temptations of immoral living. The younger generations are desperate for intimacy and long for rich deep relationships. However, in the end, their experience with sex is the opposite of true intimacy.

The result is despair, pain, and emptiness which are the inevitable consequence of immoral living. What can we do?

- We need to teach our children the Bible's perspective on sexuality.
- We need to help them understand why God's plan for sexuality is true intimacy and far more satisfying than what our culture is offering.

- We need to emphasize the devastating results of living outside of God's ideal.
- We need to teach them that research shows that cohabitating brings less happiness than marriage[68] and results in a greater chance for divorce.[69]
- We can share the statistics of divorce and the data that talks about the pain and suicidal tendencies of those who are wrestling over gender issues.
- We can show them God's perspective on the value of life, that all life is valued, and that life begins at conception.
- We need to talk about the devastating effects of abortion and the pain of those who have experienced it. Abortion isn't about freedom of choice; abortion has devalued life. It hasn't uplifted women or improved cultural norms.

We need to help our children see the consequences of sin and help them realize that the world's way doesn't work. We must show our kids that God's way is the best way—the only way.

Restoring Trust: Practice What you Preach

This generation of adults is one that values integrity and honesty. Why be involved in an organization that preaches love and truth but fails to show it? However, the statistics are alarming.

- Twenty percent of the "nones" who walked away say it is because they became disillusioned.[70]
- Thirty-six percent of Gen Z and Gen Alpha say the church has hypocrites.[71]

- Sixty-six percent of skeptics say that church scandals and abuse turned many of them away from belief in God.[72]

These are only their perceptions, but to them, perception is reality.

They are watching.

A hint of hypocrisy is all they need to see, and they are turned off.

> They observe church leaders who say one thing and do another. They see church focusing on power, politics, and money, or they experience the trauma of a church split, or the moral failure of a leader. Disillusionment follows, and they make the decision that the church (and by extension, God) are at worst, not for real, and at best are not relevant.

It's not worth their time.

Why would they continue to be involved with an organization that says one thing and does another?

Some perceive their church behaving more like a country club, caring about no one outside their group.

Others see a church arguing over something as simple as the color of the carpet while war, poverty, and disease wipe out thousands of lives.

Does any of this sound familiar?

The hypocrisy continues at home where they see their parents playing "church", attending because it's the social, acceptable thing to do, but displaying no evidence of their faith at home during the week. Instead, the worship songs are replaced with cursing and gossip, the Bible never opened.

We can't fool the next generation.

The result is they turn away, believing that the answers to the world's pain must lie elsewhere.

As a church, we must prioritize unity.

The church is not perfect, and there will always be sin because we are all sinners. No one knows that better than we do.

But we also know that it is better to be on the ark with the smelly animals than outside!

It stinks sometimes, but regardless of the stink inside, it beats the heck out of what is going on outside.

We must teach our kids to keep their eyes and their focus on the perfect person, Jesus, not on the imperfection they see around them.

> *By this all will know that you are My disciples, if you have love for one another.* (John 13:35)

Another perception of the church is that we are negative, judgmental, hypocritical, and disconnected from real issues in the community. We may know that is not true, but does the community around us?

Nothing is more important than our reputation in the community. We need to be speaking more about what we support than what we're against.

Why not use your platform to spotlight local organizations, non-profits, and businesses? Twenty-seven percent of non-Christian families say the church has no significant impact in the community.[73] We can do better.

Show that you're for others, not just for yourself.

Get involved in local community organizations so you can better understand the real issues in the community. Imagine if the church joined the local Chamber of Commerce or participated in the local school council for up-close involvement in the community. It might help us to truly understand the needs of our community.[74]

This kind of action requires work, time, and sacrifice. Getting involved in community, schools, orphanages or homeless shelters takes time and effort. Many believers prefer to just attend church on Sundays, but if we want to change the culture of our communities, we need to be engaged. Is it possible?

We might need to rethink and redefine what it means to be a follower of Christ.

> *Live such good lives among the pagans that, though they accuse you of doing wrong, they may see your good deeds and glorify God on the day he visits us.* (1 Pet. 2:12 NIV)

How can we counteract a culture that no longer believes in truth? How do we respond to the relativism that is rampant in our world?

We must exemplify a life worth watching.

As believers, our responsibility is to demonstrate truth by modeling a life that invites questions and builds credibility. We need to live out God's truth in a way that they cannot ignore. Take the absolute truth of Scripture and live it out in your own home, with your family, and at your church. The world may not be drawn to your words, but they won't be able to ignore your good works.

> *Let your light shine before others, so that they may see your good **works** and give glory to your Father who is in heaven."* (Matt. 5:16 ESV; emphasis mine)

Unfortunately, it's often difficult, if not impossible, to see the difference between believers and unbelievers. We must address our own issues.

Thirty percent of 18 to 30-year-old couples in the church are living together.[75]

Sixty-five percent of women who have an abortion identify as having some sort of Christian background.[76]

Does that sound like salt and light living to you?

We could learn much from the life of Daniel. His character was above reproach and was evident to those around him, so much so that the king decided to elevate him to a position of leadership over the entire kingdom.

> *Now Daniel so distinguished himself among the administrators and the satraps* ***by his exceptional qualities*** *that the king planned to set him over the whole kingdom.* (Dan. 6:3 NIV; emphasis mine)

He lived his faith.

He refused to eat defiled food (Daniel 2).

He faced the threat of death when he refused to stop praying (Daniel 6).

He was salt and light in his world. How can we be salt and light in ours?

When we meet people who see truth differently, instead of arguing and attacking their beliefs and ideas, we need to demonstrate a lifestyle that is consistent with what we believe, and we need to teach our children to do the same.

Restoring Belief: Teach the "Why?"

There is a new name for those Gen Z and Gen Alphas who have abandoned their faith—the "nones." Their claim to fame is that they have "no religion."

They no longer believe.

Either God doesn't exist or He doesn't matter.

The "nones" are now the fastest growing group in the United States, and surprisingly, 78 percent of them admit that they actually grew up in church.[77]

- Thirteen percent of Gen Z kids say they are atheists; 37 percent say you can't know for sure if God is real; and 58 percent say there is more than one way to God.[78]
- Twenty-six percent view the Bible as a book of fables, legends and history[79] and devastatingly, 19 percent say they don't believe in God.[80]
- Of the 81 percent who believe in God, half of them say that the "god' they believe in is not the God of the Bible.[81]

These statistics are both alarming and depressing.

Why do kids turn away from the faith?

What causes them to say, do, and believe the exact opposite of what they once embraced?

There is no one-size-fits-all answer. Perhaps it is a combination of things. A different focus or a different method? A different priority?

One thing is certain: we need to be teaching the "why" behind our beliefs. Why is the Bible trustworthy? Why is it worth following Jesus? How do we know this all makes a difference in the end? The world is taking every opportunity to undermine what they have learned at church and from godly leaders, and we must find a way to restore biblical authority in their thinking.

> Our entire culture (including secular schools) is aggressively teaching the apologetics of evolution and secular humanism. They teach our students how to defend a humanistic worldview, and they model that worldview. They show all

> the reasons that what they are teaching is supposedly true. The secularists are teaching our children how to defend the secular faith, and connecting it to the real world—and here we are in churches teaching wonderful Bible stories and reinforcing in their minds that they can believe the secularists and that the Bible is not really connected to the real world. No wonder we are losing them . . . Unless the facts behind the Christian faith are clearly and convincingly communicated in a way that students can learn and remember, their faith will not stand the assault of doubt from the world . . . Faith that is not founded on fact will ultimately falter in the storm of secularism that our students face every day.[82]

This is a quote from Answers in Genesis, a group who has prioritized apologetics in their materials. Imagine if we ran our lives and our ministries like the world, "aggressively teaching the apologetics of the Bible, defending our godly worldview, and modeling that worldview." Teaching, defending, and modeling sounds like a recipe for success.

The next sentence is key: "connecting it to the real world." These are some serious goals.

Wouldn't it be great if we were answering the questions that many in our world are asking?

We need to do that.

Our children must be able to defend their Christian faith and answer the questions raised by our very vocal world.

We are commanded in Scripture to be prepared to give answers for our beliefs.

> *But sanctify the Lord God in your hearts, and always be ready to give a defense to everyone who asks you a reason for the hope that is in you, with meekness and fear.* (1 Pet. 3:15)

But what about our children?

We must include this in our teaching, both at home and at church. Satan is engaging in an all-out war for the hearts and minds of this generation. If their beliefs are solidified by the age of nine, we cannot wait until they're older to begin answering their questions. George Barna says, "In the race to a child's heart, the first one there wins."[83]

Why should our kids believe the Bible? Perhaps we cannot imagine a world where our kids would question the most foundational truths, but the reality is that they are. They are walking away and landing in a big, dark world, unprepared for the onslaught of questions and arguments for which they have not been equipped to answer. Surrounded by peers and teachers who relentlessly pound at their shallow beliefs, they leave—the church, their faith, and worse still, God.

It's time to take action. Support your teaching with "why's" and "how's."

> Discuss the apparent contradictions that they will eventually face. Bible stories without principles and application will result in little more than a recollection of children's tales.

This generation needs a solid biblical worldview to enable them to resist the battle for their minds.

In addition to teaching biblical stories, we need to be sharing our own personal life stories and testimonies which demonstrate how God is working in people's lives. We should be sharing stories and answers to prayer.

> Be real, transparent, and vulnerable, and willing to share some of the struggles we face and how God has helped us face them. These stories are irrefutable, provide hope, and display the evidence of God's power to overcome difficulties.

Perhaps bring in a speaker who struggled with post abortion issues, or someone who has struggled with a pornography addiction. Talk about the pain of divorce, and share the testimony of someone who has wrestled with transgender issues.

Try God and See

With the number of "nones" on the rise, it is critical that we demonstrate what believing in God means. Children need to have their own personal experience of God. The lessons they are hearing must travel those crucial 12 inches from the head to the heart. Head knowledge ABOUT God must lead to a relationship WITH God. The faith of their parents and teachers must become THEIR faith.

Why not try challenging your class to test the promises of God? Rather than just teaching that God answers prayer, keep a classroom journal of their prayer requests and watch to see how God responds.

When we began our first mid-week program, my then 14-year-old daughter confidently decided to pray that nine girls would sign up for her 3rd-5th Grade small group. I told her, (foolishly as it turns out), that I didn't think we'd get that many since it was our first year. I would have been thrilled if she had three or four, and I didn't want to see her disappointed. However, she was determined and began to pray.

By the last week of registration, she had five signed up, which

I thought was great! She kept praying, and by the night before our grand opening, her group had grown to seven. I was super excited, but she was still wanting more, so she kept praying. Thirty minutes before we began our first night, I received a phone call from a parent asking if it was too late to bring her children. You guessed it—two older girls, and now my daughter had 9 in her group.

Her prayers were answered, and it's something she has never forgotten.

Years ago, another young girl attended church with her neighbor family and after learning about Jesus, she trusted Him for salvation. She wanted her parents to hear the good news, too, so she invited them to attend with her. When your seven-year-old invites you to church, it's very difficult to say "no", and her parents joined her, albeit grudgingly. They, too, heard the gospel and shortly after, trusted Christ also.

That young girl is still walking with the Lord. She experienced God answering her prayers.

If we can show how God can make a difference—move our teaching from the theoretical to the practical, from principle to application—perhaps He will become more real to them.

Children who have grown up believing what their parents have told them will eventually come to a place in their lives where they must choose to adopt those beliefs for themselves. If they are not seeing the relevance of their faith and it being modeled by their parents and leaders, why should they continue? We must help our children experience God for themselves.

We know the answer! Jesus Christ is the answer! He's the answer to all of life's issues. Still, we must ask ourselves the difficult questions and find a way to share Him in a language that our kids will understand.

The fireflies are glowing.

Let's teach our children to identify their glow.

Let's equip them to distinguish light from darkness.

Let's begin to address the struggles that our kids and their parents are facing.

Let's do our part to make this world a wonderful world for our children.

We can change our Happy Meal toy without compromising our message (or, 'our burger and fries'). Let's restore belief and trust. Let's become RELEVANT again.

10

Sharpen Your Axe: Evaluate Everything

Children's ministry can feel like a never-ending treadmill of work. Stopping that treadmill to learn something new might seem like an impossible assignment. However, pushing the pause button to evaluate your ministry and think about your direction might not only save you an abundance of heartache but lead to greater and long-term success.

There is an obscure verse in the Bible which teaches the principle of taking time to sharpen your tools for a more effective result.

> *If the ax is dull and its edge unsharpened, more strength is needed, but skill will bring success.* (Eccl. 10:10 NIV)

Do you see its point?

Have you ever tried to chop wood with a dull blade? It requires much greater energy and results in much less effectiveness.

We might be spinning our wheels with the sweat pouring off our brows, trying to do anything that we can think of to reach and retain our kids, but are we being effective?

In other words, work smarter not harder.[84]

I read stories of churches who have organized huge fall festivals with hundreds of people attending but after it's over are still asking the question, "How do you keep the ones that came?" So much effort and money expended for a very small return.

Maybe we need to sharpen our axe?

If you don't have a clear vision and purpose, you need to stop long enough to sharpen your tools so that you are not swinging with a dull edge, making more sweat than progress.

There is nothing worse than working hard and feeling like you end up making little to no impact. If your ministry feels this way, it might be time for an evaluation.

Evaluate Your Church

If you have noticed the hemorrhaging of family and kids from your ministry, and are realizing that you might need to make a few adjustments, there are some essentials which must be in place before you can hope to be successful. The first order of business is ensuring that you have the support of the church.

It's easy to find churches which outwardly agree that children's ministry is important, but when the reality brings to light an inadequate budget, low visibility and a lack of volunteers, children's ministry becomes a much lower priority than was originally proclaimed.

How is the perspective at your church?

- Does the budget reflect a minimum of effort and resources (until a crisis occurs or people complain)?

- Is it necessary for you, as the leader of your ministry, to make constant appeals for finances, resources, space, and volunteers?
- Is children's ministry valued by your church leaders and frequently spoken of from the platform on Sundays?

You are facing an uphill battle if the only time your members hear or think about children's ministry is if they drop a kid off for Sunday School or happen to walk by a classroom door.

> In most churches, there is little sense of urgency about children's ministry. A leaky roof in a church creates a sense of urgency. A broken air conditioner in a Texas summer creates an immediate action. But underinvestment in children's ministry is accepted in many churches as something we'll just have to live with.[85]

Ask yourself, is the ministry valued, or regarded merely as a support ministry for "childcare"?

> Too often children's ministry takes a backseat to other ministries, or is viewed as "childcare" designed to keep the parents happy and kids occupied.

Is it seen primarily as a way to keep the kids safe and entertained to enable parents to participate in the "real" ministries of the church?

- Is the senior pastor endorsing the value of reaching children and promoting the priority of the children's department?

- Is the church leadership working to help equip the ministry with quality leaders?

If not, it will be difficult to convince the church at large that the task is more than childcare. You will need the support of the congregation, staff, and leaders. It cannot be seen as optional. You must have these people fully on board! When you evaluate your church's perception of the children's ministry, what do you see?

Evaluate Your Ministry

We must also evaluate our actual ministry. To further add to the usual challenges of ministry, when we consider the complexities of this dark world and the complicated characteristics of this new generation, the task will seem overwhelming.

These Alphas, who seemingly snuck into our ministries while we weren't looking, bring with them another learning curve. Just when we had it nailed ministering to the Gen Z'ers, along comes a completely different group!

> Evaluating your ministry in light of an ever-changing audience is critical.

What are you doing now that is new or different from last year? Five years ago? Ten years ago?

- Is the children's ministry growing or stagnant?
- Are you holding their attention or seeing eyes staring off into space?
- Have you done a curriculum evaluation recently?

- Are you trying to implement something new and creative?
- Are you experimenting with ideas you learned from networking with other leaders?
- Have you been to a Children's Ministry Conference in the last few years?

You may be thinking, 'if I do all that, I'll be exhausted!' Maybe so, but you will also likely advance your ministry and be more successful at calling Alpha kids to come inside!

> Churches that refuse to change, that refuse to focus on equipping the next generation and that refuse to let the next generation have leadership roles, are signing the autopsy papers for their church.[86]

If children and families are disappearing, maybe it's time to do an evaluation.

Evaluate Your Motives

Whether your church is big or small, old or new, we all have something in common. We all share the same mission of reaching kids and families. We all serve the same God who calls, guides, provides, and produces the fruit in our ministries.

> While it might appear glamourous from the outside, the truth is that you are in a position that gives no guarantee of the outcome, whilst waging war against the powerful enemy of this world.

Even if you give it your all, there is no promise of temporal success.

Sure, there may come a measure of victory. The LORD may bless your efforts. Yet we do well to always remember that "*it is God who works in you both to will and to do for His good pleasure*" (Phil. 2:13).

He is the One who grants success.

Our efforts alone will never accomplish His will without His intervention.

No doubt you have felt the sting of being the lowest on the totem pole in the staff meeting.

- You request a room but something "more important" kicks you out.
- The worship team arrives for practice while you are trying to run a midweek program. Unannounced scaffolding is erected in the foyer, meaning that you can't have the scheduled Wednesday night program, but nobody told you that!
- You're forced to use church management software that is horrendous when it's applied in children's ministry without being consulted.

I understand, I've been there.

While we are not in it for the money, it doesn't feel good discovering the well-hidden fact that your salary is significantly lower than the "pastoral" staff.

When the explanation given is that the "real pastors" have a greater responsibility and are required to be available to make hospital visits in the middle of the night, that probably won't quite explain the discrepancy.

We know all too well how hard children's pastors work.

We know how many volunteers we oversee.

We know how many families are in our database.

Do you see other staff having time to play badminton in the worship room and go out to lunch multiple times each week with volunteers?

Have you felt the isolation from the adult members of the church because your responsibilities have prevented you from being able to attend services?

These are some of the challenges that children's ministry leaders face on a daily basis.

> Children's Ministry is hard, and unfortunately, most of us will have to wait until heaven for our reward. It's easy to slip into the victim mentality when you focus on the negatives and when it feels like you're working so hard for so little.

We must remember that we are working for an audience of One. If we want to survive, we must, as far as we are able, remember who it is that we are trying to please.

> *And whatever you do, do it heartily, as to the Lord and not to men, knowing that from the Lord you will receive the reward of the inheritance; for you serve the Lord Christ.* (Col. 3:23-24)

Evaluate Yourself

The last area that we need to check on is ourselves.

Working so hard with no guarantee or control over success is hard enough, but to make it even more challenging, the life of a children's pastor is one of the most wide-ranging, relentless positions in the church. The job is never finished.

We move from season to season with no breaks. We prepare for Easter and the spring festival, and once it's over we move immediately into planning for the summer. Summer camp is exhausting, but followed by fun family events, then it's back to school. Fall is right behind, followed by Christmas, and we begin all over again.

We work on recruiting, training and managing adult and teen volunteers, counseling and loving children through all development and behavioral stages, and encouraging, equipping and appeasing parents.

Then we have those never-ending administrative tasks like developing and maintaining security policies, scheduling, calendars/databases, planning and coordinating camps, family activities and special events, check in systems, evaluating, buying and organizing curriculum, music and supplies, planning and administering a budget, designing and editing newsletters, and maintaining websites and advertising.

Whilst doing all of that, we must also keep the senior pastor as well as the janitor happy, answering voice mails, e-mails, and snail mail and not to mention the countless meetings with donuts you don't need that seem more soporific than helpful.

Phew! It's exhausting just thinking about it.

> In spite of this, most of us are underpaid, underappreciated, understaffed, overworked and overloaded, covered in glitter and goldfish crumbs.

Someone recently posted on Facebook and said it this way:

I feel as though I eat, drink, and breathe Children's Ministry, like my mind never turns off. It's a constant checking of emails, making social media posts, texting this parent or that, creating this craft, dropping off packages to a child's home. It just never ends.

If you are struggling, join the club. Ministry is tough.

Within six months of beginning the children's director position at my church, we had grown from 30 children and volunteers to 80 children, 75 volunteers, and approximately 120 parents. It was a mid-size church, and I was only one person. From the minute I arrived at the office until I turned out the last light and locked the doors, I was running at 100mph.

If you've been in ministry for any length of time, you will no doubt have experienced at one time or other a loss of joy, a short-fuse, a feeling of isolation and exhaustion, to name just a few. Going head-to-head with the devil is a hair-raising experience, and you most definitely need to equip yourself daily with the armor of God if you hope to survive.

- How are you doing?
- How is your relationship with the Lord?
- Are you spending time with him daily?
- Are you exercising, resting, prioritizing family time?
- Do you have a life outside of your ministry?
- Do you have any friends outside of your children's ministry?
- How are YOU doing?

Perhaps you need to stop and do a personal evaluation before looking at the bigger picture. Burnout is a very real danger in ministry, and it's very difficult to recover. Remember that preventative medicine is best and "an ounce of prevention is worth a pound of cure."

If you are at the end of your rope or asking yourself, "How did I get myself into this?" remember God's promise:

> *Therefore, we do not lose heart. Even though our outward man is perishing, yet the inward man is being renewed day by day. For our light affliction, which is but for a moment, is working for us a far more exceeding and eternal weight of glory, while we do not look at the things which are seen, but at the things which are not seen. For the things which are seen are temporary, but the things which are not seen are eternal.* (2 Cor. 4:16-18)

> *Therefore, my beloved brethren, be steadfast, immovable, always abounding in the work of the Lord, knowing that your labor is not in vain in the Lord.* (1 Cor. 15:58)

Be Willing to Learn and Change

Many kid's ministry leaders have little to no Bible or ministry training, education, or experience.[87] They are often recruited from the current volunteer team because they had demonstrated faithfulness and passion. I had been involved previously with youth ministry, church planting, women's ministry, and a variety of administrative roles but never formally with children.

My original training was in secondary education, so working with "little people" was not a part of my agenda. But God had other plans, and so I had a huge learning curve.

Because so few of us have much in the way of formal training in the work we are doing, we scramble to learn as much as we can. It may be a conference here, a half-read book there, articles, blogs, and lots of conversations with friends.

If we want to remain effective and relevant, we must schedule and protect the time to do it.

- We need to study and understand the current culture—google the current movies, trends, and video games.
- We must prioritize learning by participating in some of the many available conferences and programs, and when you do, identify the top two best ideas to implement!
- We need to network with other local children's pastors for support and encouragement and join the social media pages, which specialize in kid's ministry, to find creative ideas and suggestions.
- We should be reading good books on the topics where we need help. The best leaders never stop learning.

The very fact that you're investing time reading this book indicates that you're open to staying current and making adjustments.

> Say hello to this current generation and get to know them. Their needs are different, they learn differently, and what they need from your children's ministry is different than the kids before them.

Attempting to discover generational trends before it's too late is a notoriously frustrating proposition and it feels like the time that we spend reading books and learning is precious time that we could otherwise be investing in making a difference in kid's lives.

However, if we stop and evaluate, we might discover that the ministry we've created for the last generation is actually now outdated and no longer relevant.

How then do we as children's ministers keep up with the trends that impact children from generation to generation?

Start by taking a long, hard look at what you are doing and how you are doing it. Be courageous enough to change what needs to be changed, stop what is ineffective and needs to be stopped, and start what needs to be started. Christian education programs from years ago might not need to be eradicated, but they certainly need to be renovated. Always keep asking, "How could that be done better?"

Reinvent. Revitalize. Renew.

Unfortunately, with the ever-changing culture, this need is ongoing. I get it.

We are in the trenches with no time to modify anything.

There is no margin in our schedules for change.

But we must.

We can't lose any more kids.

We need to be effective in what we are doing.

> One of the biggest mistakes we can make is to keep repeating programs that were successful in the past, not stopping to take a breath and evaluate how we might be able to be more effective, and not understanding or giving consideration to the changing audience we are trying to reach.

Instead, they disappear—families, kids, one by one . . . a never-ending hemorrhage.

A Word to the Wise

Implementing change is difficult, challenging, and might even seem impossible, but in some cases, it might be necessary if you are to see growth.

We like to feel in control and we are, for the most part, creatures of habit. There are often strong connections with the old and a lack of trust in the new. It is wise to show respect for the past, balancing the old with the new, and implementing change gradually. Call it a "pilot program" or an "experiment" to give people time to adjust to the idea. Experiments allow for the possibility of failure; let your leaders know that failure is OK. That's how we learn.

Most of us have heard one version or another of Thomas Edison's famous quote about failure and inventing the light bulb. When a reporter asked him, "How did it feel to fail 1,000 times?" Edison replied, "I didn't fail 1,000 times. The light bulb was an invention with 1,000 steps."

"Great success is built on failure, frustration, even catastrophe." We shouldn't be afraid to try new things.

That is how we learn.

The best way to introduce people to change is to first help them see why change is needed. Keep attendance records and lists of families who have disappeared. Let your church leaders see the loss in black and white. Then work on suggested changes together.

Remember that although you can never please everyone, forcing ideas on people with no regard for other's opinions and feelings is a recipe for disaster. Instead, guide others to see the current reality and need to change.

Every program has a peak where it reaches its best years. Once it peaks, it begins to decline in effectiveness. Letting go of a program which has been around for years is hard.

The timing of that change is critical.

Anticipating and seeing the need in advance is ideal, but you might be the only one that sees it. Reacting to the obvious signs of need is easier, but the tradeoff is that you will lose some momentum.

Once you reach crisis level, the need for change will be obvious to most but will come at a greater cost.

The ideal time for change is mid-way between anticipating the need and reacting.

Beware: Watch out for the "sacred cows."

These are the programs, furnishings, or resources that have branded on the front "Don't touch under threat of death."

Make sure that you have the full support of the leadership before making changes to them. This is especially difficult if you're new and full of creativity, but gradual implementation is never a bad idea.

Some churches and ministries react negatively to change because they never have. It can be helpful to change things every now and again just so people become accustomed to it.

In our church-planting days, my husband and I would sometimes change the order of service, just to keep things from seemingly being set in stone.

Sometimes, we would sit on the opposite side of the worship room to avoid having hard and fast seating.

In the long run, it can help create a "culture of change."

Change is usually a healthy thing!

The key is developing trust with your team and communicating well so that change can be initiated early on.

Unfortunately, you should expect some resistance and even be willing to lose some people. If you are receiving strong objections from key people or the majority of your team is unsupportive, sometimes it is wiser to wait (Ps. 27:14).

Remember, that if we want to be effective, we need a sharp axe. One way to ensure this is regular evaluation.

- Evaluate the church, your ministry, your motives, and yourself.

- Be willing to learn and change.
- Be open to suggestions, and dare I say, even criticism.
- Always be asking, "How can we improve? How could we have done this better?"

Then we can rest, knowing that we have done our best, and the rest is up to God.

PART THREE

HELP: Change the Plan

Everyone knows how fireflies got their name, but many people don't know how these insects (which are actually beetles) produce their signature glow. Fireflies are distinguished by having dedicated light organs called a "lantern", which are located under their abdomen. The insects take in oxygen, combining it inside special cells with a substance called luciferin, which produces their characteristic bioluminescent glow with almost no heat.

Unique in the animal kingdom, fireflies can control their light like a switch: each firefly flashing its light in an intermittent pattern, unique to each species. Each blinking pattern is an optical signal that helps fireflies' glow to get the attention of females and find potential mates. Scientists are not sure how the insects regulate this process to turn their lights on and off, but the result is a wonder of light.

Just as fireflies exhibit their own uniqueness with their intermittent patterns of light, so do Generation Alpha display their distinctive traits. Experts will be studying them for years to come. It's not yet possible to predict exactly what they will become. Right now, we are only guessing. But even though we don't fully understand, we must begin to make plans.

We must begin to adjust to what we DO know.

We must provide the help they need to survive in the nighttime.

11

The #1 Priority: Relationships Before Everything

Kids are constantly scrolling through their phones looking for something that will capture their interests. Due to over-exposure of information, many have become jaded. Teachers today have to compete for their attention with YouTube, Instagram, Netflix, and Snapchat. How do we teach a kid who is so difficult to impress?

My advice is not to try.

I believe educators and parents can play a unique role in the lives of students by investing in their lives. While Hollywood can capture their attention for a few moments, caring adults can engage them in a way that's personal and meaningful."[88]

The reality is that the social lives of families are no longer centered around the church. Families rush in and rush out on Sundays, without any real, deep connections. Yet this is one of their greatest needs.

Without meaningful relationships in the church, they are less prone to be consistent in their attendance. If no one will even notice their absence, why should they bother to come? Instead, they fulfill that need elsewhere!

In children's ministry, we are often so determined to make our ministry more attractive and enticing that we can sometimes lose perspective. We forget that their greater need is for meaningful relationships. We get caught up in trying to impress kids with a professional quality of entertainment and technology.

Yes, excellence is important, but constant excellence is neither possible nor necessary. What these kids really need is less stuff and more relationships.

> Rather than focusing primarily on *programs*, we need to focus on *people*. Relationships are what really matters and the only thing that will really last.

We won't be remembered for the amazing graphics or high-tech lighting, but our kids will remember the teacher who cared. They will remember the teacher who prayed with them, or even better, showed up on their front doorstep on their birthday.

Small church or mega church? This is achievable in EVERY church.

And it won't take a chunk out of your budget!

Dale Hudson writes:

> Children are not desperate for our amazing, on-screen graphics. They see much better graphics all week on TV and social media. But they are desperate to see someone in their life who believes in them.
>
> Children are not desperate for our games and fun at VBS. They play in sport's leagues and have tons of other

> extracurricular activities. But they are desperate for someone who will listen . . . really listen to them.
>
> Children are not desperate for our take home papers. They are already overwhelmed by hundreds of messages that are sent their way every day. But they are desperate for someone who knows the challenges they are facing at home and cares about what they are going through.
>
> Children are not desperate for our quiet seat prizes. They have plenty of trinkets and access to candy already. But they are desperate for someone who will sit with them and quietly pray for their prayer needs.[89]

Kids need to know that someone loves them, someone cares about them, and that they matter!

Always remember this old mantra: "Kids don't care how much we know until they know how much we care."

For children to grow and understand God's love, they need to know they're loved, accepted, and cared for by those who are the messengers.

Children want to feel welcome, and meaningful relationships are key.

Consistent Leaders are a Must

When I began as a children's ministry director, there were no consistent volunteers in our church. Everyone rotated, teaching once each month, and there were only enough volunteers to schedule one adult in each class. None of them knew the kid's names, and the parents had no idea who the teachers would be each week.

This kind of scheduling is less than ideal, and worse, ineffective.

It is impossible to develop any level of relationship with the kids or the families when you only see them once a month for an hour.

- No consistency with the lessons.
- No uniformity with classroom management.
- No knowledge of who needs follow-up.

I have never heard of a Girl Scout troop or a sports team asking for volunteers to only serve once a month, but here we were, with once-a-month volunteers. And it wasn't because we were small. We had two services with an average attendance of 400 people.

We needed a team.

My first priority was to *find that team*—people who cared enough to serve consistently.

I was desperate.

I met with the senior pastor, and we looked through the entire church directory, scouring (at that point) for any warm bodies that might fill the gaps. At the very least, we needed two adults in every class, so I was willing for any able volunteer. I would concern myself with in-depth training later.

I sent out a semi-personal email to each one we identified as a possible volunteer (in other words, I inserted their name at the top!) and asked for their help. Out of approximately 160 requests, I had 80 who responded. Our ministry was now out of danger.

Once I had enough leaders to safely run the classes, I began to watch and discern who might be gifted in the area of teaching. I spent time talking with each person and found out who had offered to serve just because they wanted to help me out and who genuinely had a passion for children. I began to ask some to serve twice a month and that enabled me to release some to other areas of service.

After a year, I challenged the team to step up and serve every week.

For churches with only one service, rotating your leaders is a necessity. When we were church planting and our church was small, we had no choice but to rotate. So, we chose to have short-term rotations where our volunteers would serve for one month every quarter, and we provided them recorded copies of the services so they could still hear the messages each week.

Another option would be to use two teams which serve every other week. The teams can coordinate with each other, and this would allow for some consistency.

I was able to recruit twelve people the first year who were willing to be "full-time" leaders. Another four offered to serve twice a month. That meant that nearly every class had at least one adult who served them each week. The other assistant still rotated monthly, but it made an enormous difference to have some consistency. I began to work more specifically with those twelve and kept my eyes open for another eight.

Whatever your situation is, try as much as possible to keep your team regular and consistent to enable them to develop some depth in their relationships with the kids.

Love Them

I remember many times when I've visited a church and felt alone. You don't know anyone, and you stand there awkwardly, watching groups of people chatting but not with you. You try to smile and appear friendly, but they don't even see you.

My personal strategy then is to find the nearest bulletin board and pretend to be busy reading, trying desperately to look like I belong. You want to shrink between the floorboards so that you're not so obvious.

What you really need is for a friendly face to approach you and say "welcome"—anything to help you feel more comfortable.

Children experience similar feelings when they visit for the first time. They may feel alone, unnoticed, or awkward.

Our task is to love them!

Our goal should be to implement a strategy to alleviate those first-time jitters and fears. Train your leaders to watch for visiting families, and be ready to incorporate them into the group. There's nothing worse than having to read the bulletin board!

Your job is to shepherd every child. Whether or not your title says "Pastor," that's what you are.

> *Keep watch over yourselves and all the flock of which the Holy Spirit has made you overseers. Be shepherds of the church of God, which he bought with his own blood.* (Acts 20:28)

> *Be shepherds of God's flock that is under your care, watching over them—not because you must, but because you are willing, as God wants you to be; not pursuing dishonest gain, but eager to serve.* (1 Pet. 5:2 NIV)

Yes, our material is important. We need it to be engaging and to communicate all the right foundational truths. But it's the people and the relationships that are key.

> The number one priority needs to be relationships before everything. Love them! Love them! Love them!

Children are craving real relationships, and that should be our goal.

Not amazing programs, eye-catching VBS backdrops, or flashing lights.

Yes, those things are great, but loving our kids is greater and will reap unfathomable results.

Try an experiment.

When you see a child on their device, offer to play a game with them or do something fun together.

Often, kids are on their phones or iPads because of a lack of emotional connectedness with the adults around them.

It's our unavailability or lack of attention as parents and educators that makes them default to the easy stimulation of a screen. Ouch!

There are very few kids who will remain engaged to a screen if an adult is ready to connect, play, listen, or do a fun activity with them.[90] Don't just assume a child is "on their device" because they don't have a desire to be engaged.

Whenever possible, maintain small group ratios to provide greater interaction with the kids.

- Begin with an icebreaker game each week to help kids connect.
- Get directly involved and play games with them; don't just stand in the back corner and watch.
- Appoint "classroom hosts" who sit with first time visitors.
- Follow up with children who miss two programs in a row.
- Send a handwritten personal postcard to visitors, absent kids, birthday kids—and remember other special occasions.

- If a child tells you his favorite candy bar, take note and surprise him on his birthday.
- Get down on their level and make direct eye contact.

When Walt Disney was designing and building the main street of Disney Land, he told his engineers to get down on their knees as they drew up the plans. He wanted to make sure they were at the same eye level as the children who would come to the park.

Imagine your leaders kneeling on the floor to welcome each child with a smile and a high five,

"I am so glad you're here."

"I've been waiting all week to see you!"

Perhaps assign a leader (or even better a teen helper) standing by the classroom door and offer high fives to kids as they come in.

Come early, leave late.

What if you came 30 minutes earlier and hung out with the kids before service starts?

What if, instead of rushing out as soon as service is over, you hung around and spent some time investing in that child who doesn't get picked up by their parents until 20 minutes after service is over?

- Ask about how they are doing at school. Even better, offer to serve in some capacity at their school.
- Find out what they like, their interests, what they watch and listen to.
- Be in touch with their families so you know when kids are going through tough times.
- Attend their soccer game or practice, or dance recital.

- Organize to meet a couple of parents and their kids and buy them all ice cream during the week.

Be the leader who cares. Love them. Love them. Love them.

Love Them All

There is *no place* in ministry for playing favorites.

There is no denying that some kids are easier to love than others. Every church will have the cute little girls who are always smiling or the cool boys who are in line to win the latest popularity contest. But there will also be the awkward, shy kids standing in the corner, or the poorly dressed one who could use a bath and a hair brush.

Which do you find easier to engage in conversation? We need to love them all.

I was volunteering in a church recently and it was interesting to observe the leadership as they interacted with the kids before the program began. To my dismay, it was the outgoing, well-dressed, "popular" kids (or the misbehaving ones) that received the majority of the high fives and fist bumps. The key leaders showed real preference when choosing which kids to talk to, gravitating to the attractive and well-liked kids. The shy, quiet, more awkward kids were standing off to the side often alone and no doubt would have been reading the bulletin board if there had been one nearby.

We must always be careful to equally proportion our time amongst all the children.

Don't fall into the trap of just loving the easy ones.

We are called to love the unlovely.

We must love them all.

> [You] *must not show favoritism. Suppose a man* [or child] *comes into your meeting wearing a gold ring and fine clothes,*

> *and a poor man in filthy old clothes also comes in. If you show special attention to the man wearing fine clothes and say, "Here's a good seat for you," but say to the poor man, "You stand there" or "Sit on the floor by my feet," have you not discriminated among yourselves? . . . But if you show favoritism, you sin . . .* (James 2:1-4, 9 NIV)

The face of our children's ministry will continue to be increasingly diverse, both multiculturally and socially.

We must be welcoming and engaging to all children and their families.

Use the languages, music, and images from all different cultures represented in your community for special music, teaching, and print communication.

Learn about the values of the cultures you minister alongside.

Will you love your children in their language? It just might be the missing link to draw them back in.

Remember the #1 priority: relationships before everything.

They need a friend more than they need to be "wowed."

Let's include them all.

Let's understand them all.

Let's love our kids, and love them all!

12

Preteens: The Awkward "Middle Child"

Ah! Preteens!

Too grown up for the children's ministry, they are tossed to the youth ministry.

But they are not ready for the issues and activities of youth, and they don't fit in with the teenagers. The youth think of the preteens as immature and silly, and feel that they don't belong. They guzzle all of the snacks, don't listen to instructions, and just whine and complain all the time. At least, that is their perception.

The preteens feel that the kids below them are immature and silly, that they have grown out of singing songs and making crafts. So, what do we do with them?

We've known for a while that 75% of young adults are leaving the church, but do we realize that the age they are leaving is becoming younger? The tendency now is for them to leave during middle school. If that is true, it means that this preteen age group is a crucial time and we must capitalize on it, making it as effective as possible.

> These preteen years might be the last chance that we have to curb this ebbing tide. We don't want to be left fishing at the shore when all of the fish have been swept out to the ocean.

Churches are beginning to understand that this age group requires a specialized emphasis. They have their own unique set of needs and challenges.

It is not as simple as treating preteen ministry as a mini or early youth ministry. Preteens are neither children nor youth, and to combine this age group with middle school is extremely unwise.

Instead, we need to modify the program and atmosphere of this age group away from the style in children's ministry and toward something more like youth ministry. Preteens need a bridge—from kid's ministry to youth. Help them prepare for the transition by adding some youth elements to your upper-elementary program. Otherwise, kids can have a difficult time making the adjustment.

Abstract Thinking and Cognitive Pruning

The stage of preteen or "tweenager" is a time of enormous change. The first twelve years of life are a time of great receptivity, but the preteen years might actually be the most receptive of all.

There are two times when a human goes through tremendous neurological growth: one is just after infancy and the other is around 10, 11, and 12.[91]

> [During these years] . . . a child's brain is getting ready for adulthood and becomes malleable again. If you were to

> look at a scan of a two-year-old's or a three-year-old's brain and compare it to a scan of an 11-year-old's, the scans look the same. Very similar monumental developmental shifts are happening . . . [92]

This is the time for significant learning. Preteens are beginning to think in more complex ways and are beginning to shift from concrete thinking to abstract thinking, and this opens the door for a completely different learning style.

This is the time to answer the questions and allow for plenty of discussion. Resist the urge to be the "teacher." Think along the lines of "coach" or "facilitator".

- Try engaging your preteens with more discussion. Use questions to draw them out.
- Talk about the movie and fashion trends when discussing Daniel's temptation to follow the crowd.
- Talk about the fear of confronting a bully when teaching about Esther and her struggle to overcome Haman.
- Try picking up one of the various teen magazines on the market and address the current issues they are facing.

It's also when our brains get rid of what we don't need or use, a process called "cognitive pruning". During these years, preteens decide if information is worth retaining or not.

- What is worth remembering and what can I discard?
- Is church useful or not?
- Is the Bible really true or is it just a bunch of fairytales?
- Do I have time for this, or are the other interests in my life more valuable?

It's an especially critical time in their spiritual life and development.

Waning Interest

This is the time when kids begin to lose interest.

They are no longer impressed by our efforts to wow them with programs and technology—they have seen it all, and much better.

It used to be fun, but now, not so much.

Research tells us that kids used to leave when they reached adulthood, free from their parent's restraint. But now, it is earlier. Karl Bastian of Kidology says, "after high school seniors, tweens are the second largest group of people to leave the church and never come back."[93]

Drawn in by the attractions of the world, they fight their parents until they win. Parents are so fearful of losing their relationship with them that they succumb to the pressure and allow them to skip church. Sunday sports are permitted. Basketball practice takes the place of the mid-week program. There is no time for family devotions. They are finally free! They have successfully reduced their interaction with God to the occasional church service or special event.

Barna research highlights the increase in church hopping. For 27 percent of practicing Christians, "church hopping" has become the norm,[94] skipping around for special events or well-known preachers or staying home for "online church." While some exposure to church is arguably better than none, inconsistent attendance provides no real connection or regular Bible teaching, and our children are suffering.

The Need for an Older Friend

This age group has an increased desire for independence and freedom from their parents which only furthers the need for meaningful relationships in the church.

For young children, the family is the center of the universe, but friends and peer approval become increasingly influential for preteens as they begin to branch out from family and express their individuality and independence. Socially, their focal point is shifting. Cliques emerge, and fashion and friends begin to define what's "cool." They tend to be very self-conscious, self-absorbed, and egocentric, believing their feelings are unique and thinking that everyone is focused on them.

> With this increased independence from their parents, preteens tend to reach out to surrogate families to fill the void, making mentors a critical addition to their relationship circle.

Other adults, mentors, and friends can be influential allies in helping to encourage and disciple kids when it's not viable for the church or parents, or when additional support is needed. There is always room for more encouragement. In fact, advice is usually more readily accepted coming from a non-family member.

Even though we regularly attended a Bible-believing church growing up, our family was a mess. All five of us kids were exposed to a hypocritical, distant, abusive father, and my parents separated while we were in our teens. But that is not the end of the story. Amazingly, all five of us remained committed to our faith with four of us serving in full-time Christian ministry.

What made the difference?

I asked my siblings what made the difference for them. The common denominator for all of us was the influence of an encouraging friend. Each one of us has a story to tell of an adult who cared.

A friend who provided transportation to church activities.

A friend who showed an interest and cared enough to be there.

A friend who spent time answering our questions.

A friend who provided a shoulder to cry on.

For me, it was a married couple in my church.

I occasionally babysat for them and stayed overnight in their home. Other times, they invited me to dinner or took me out for an early breakfast. I was able to observe their interactions together as husband and wife and watched them as they prayed with their children at bedtime.

I carried that picture of a healthy family into my own marriage, determined to break the chain of dysfunction which I had experienced growing up. I can't imagine where I would be now without their friendship. Their investment of time quite possibly saved my life.

For my brothers, it was a senior widower who showed an interest.

He was a faithful brother in Christ from our home church in Australia who knew something of our family situation and cared enough to reach out on a consistent basis.

He would call them to check in and see how they were doing.

He would write brief letters when he was overseas with work.

He would take them out to dinner every now and then.

Eternity alone will reveal the fruit that his efforts will have produced.

It doesn't take any special talent or money . . . just an investment of love and time.

Take a moment to consider the people who have invested in your life. Who in your past cared enough to show an interest, created a safe space for you to be honest, pointed you to God's Word, and spurred you on in your spiritual growth?

Do you remember your favorite Sunday school teacher?

Did you have a mature Christian adult who walked alongside you?

> Science shows that children who do well despite serious hardship have had at least one stable and committed relationship with a supportive adult. These relationships buffer children from developmental disruption and help them develop "resilience," or the set of skills needed to respond to adversity and thrive.[95]

That was certainly true in our case. Barna agrees.

> When comparing twenty somethings who remained active in their faith beyond high school and twenty somethings who dropped out of church, the Barna study uncovered a significant difference between the two. Those who stay were twice as likely to have a close personal friendship with an adult inside the church.[96]

Unfortunately, "nearly half of all preteens admit that they don't have any role models."[97] Imagine if the church was able to assist by providing godly role models to these children.

Consider investing in your students during the week and not just on a Sunday.

- Volunteer at the local elementary school to help in a classroom where many of your kids attend school or serve where needed.
- Go to school awards ceremonies, talent shows, or special events.
- Why not invite three kids from your group to go grocery shopping with you or go and watch their baseball game? All with parental consent and approval of course.

Remember, the #1 priority is relationships.

I still remember my Sunday school teacher.

I don't remember the lessons, but I remember that she loved me.

The relationship we develop with our kids might be the difference between them succumbing to the attractions of our ever-darkening world and instead, choosing to run to the light of God's love.

This preteen stage is a critical time.

We need to prioritize this age group, and not see them as the awkward "middle child".

13

How Alphas Learn: An Active Learning Approach

Alphas' minds are inquisitive. They are a hands-on generation, learning best by doing and experiencing. Unfortunately, most of our teaching historically has been traditional and linear.

Even though we know that the old-school, up-front teaching style has the worst learning retention rate,[98] it is still the most commonly used approach, probably because it requires the least effort on the part of the teacher.

No doubt you grew up as I did, learning with this monologue format. We sat quietly (some of the time) while the teacher did all of the talking. It will be our natural inclination to teach the same way, but we need to see ourselves as a facilitator and guide, rather than a lecturer.

This generation of children does not think or learn in the same way that previous generations did, and we need to make some changes if we hope to be effective. We need to adapt to this changing world by incorporating new teaching techniques and providing an environment that enhances our program.

> Alphas learn by engaging with the story in an experiential approach to learning, rather than merely a cerebral approach. They learn most effectively by talking, laughing, doing, and lots of opportunities to move and just be a kid rather than being forced to "sit still and be quiet."

With the issues they will be facing in the future, Alphas need to be developing their critical thinking and problem-solving skills. They need to learn to see problems from different perspectives, analyzing possible alternative solutions and then making decisions based on their own personal beliefs and individual thinking. This style of learning is even more important as your kids progress through the elementary ages.

What if our approach to teaching in children's ministry changed to match our world today?

Generation Alpha requires a new approach to teaching, but it's difficult for curriculum companies to write based on that new approach. It's also more time-consuming for Sunday school teachers to prepare that kind of lesson. So, we stay with what's easier. Perhaps we need to be reminded that we arrive at a whole new level of accountability if we take on the role of teaching kids.

> Be careful that it is the truth which you inculcate, and only that. With such a responsibility, how solemn your work becomes! . . . Remember that you are laboring for God, if you are what you profess to be. Alas! many, I fear, are far from having this serious view of the work of a Sunday-school teacher.[99]

One of the highest honors in being a children's ministry leader is being entrusted to teach children.

Ineffective teaching makes everything else in your ministry a waste of time. In order to teach well, you should know your students well. How do they learn? What stage of life are they in? What are the characteristics of their age? Teaching children is an honor and a privilege, an incredibly important responsibility, and we will reap results based upon our preparation. Prepare as though your lesson truly matters, because it does!

> *My brethren, let not many of you become teachers, knowing that we will receive a stricter judgement.* (James 3:1)

Active Learning

We need to give some thought to how we can adjust our teaching styles to complement this new generation of children. A preferable approach to the traditional up-front teacher is "Active Learning" whereby students actively participate in the learning process, as opposed to sitting quietly and listening.

Active learning takes into account how they learn, not just what they learn. Our job as teachers is to provide the environments, instruction, and opportunities that encourage that learning such as asking open-ended questions which encourage our students to think and integrating activity with the lesson and directing the learning.

> Active learning focuses on how students learn, not just on what they learn. Students are encouraged to 'think hard', rather than passively receive information from the teacher. Research shows us that it is not possible to transmit understanding to students by simply telling them what they need to know. Instead, teachers need to make sure that they challenge their students' thinking.[100]

This approach does not have to mean a complete change to your classroom practice. Sometimes it only means a small adjustment, adding time for discussion and questions.

If students are actively engaged in group discussion, will it be noisier? Probably!

If there is more physical movement, will it be chaotic? Possibly!

If you allow for questions, will your students disagree at times? It's likely!

But each of these situations is positive and mostly beneficial.

It's healthy for students to engage with questions.

It's good for students to discuss your interpretations and teaching.

Healthy discussion is beneficial for students and teachers.

Healthy discussion means that students are engaging with their teacher as a partner in their learning.

Knowing how these Alpha kids learn, we need to allow our teaching to become more prescriptive than descriptive.

- Involve them in the learning process.
- Give them a question and challenge them to find the answer.
- Allow the kids to think for themselves and resist the urge to provide all the answers.
- Allow them the joy of discovery.
- Instead of having children fill in blanks, have them brainstorm answers as you write them on the board.

Rather than leading children to the conclusion you are looking for, let them discover it on their own. We tend to remember things we've discovered ourselves for longer periods of time, and the memories will be more vivid.

- If you begin with a large group worship time, move your chairs and make circles for the discussion time.
- Charge the kids with the responsibility for discovery and create learning pods or small groups where kids can interact with other kids.
- Appoint a group leader for each of the groups and rotate the responsibility each week between the students.
- Update your teaching style and adopt a new approach that speaks the Alpha language more clearly.

More than Bedtime Stories

Jesus prioritized the use of stories when He taught and so should we. He was the Master Teacher always integrating truth with life.

> *Jesus spoke all these things to the crowd in parables* [stories]*; He did not say anything to them without using a parable.* (Matt. 13:34 NIV)

We are wired to listen to stories.

Have you ever noticed there is something about stories that captivate our attention?

Beckworth says, " . . . it is far easier for me to fall in love with a character in a story than with an exhortation or list of theological propositions about that character."[101]

The next time you are teaching, notice what happens when you tell a story. Any kind of story.

They can be stories from your childhood, stories from current news, Bible stories, or stories about heroes of the faith. The kids will zoom in with you and carefully listen.

- Let them engage with the story and consider the meaning for themselves.

- Use a variety of activities which activate the different learning styles.
- Provide time for reflection and questions.
- Use PowerPoint or a similar program to add visuals to your stories, helping to maximize interest and retention.

Generation Alpha regularly engages with videos, apps, and games facilitated by technology. YouTube is the second most popular search engine on the internet (after Google), but for Generation Alpha, it's number one.

Why would they read something when they can watch it?

Their preference for technology has resulted in short attention spans, and they favor images and fast-moving activities. They would rather watch a video about a topic instead of reading about it, so show a clip of a current movie and follow it with a discussion.

Use short teaching segments and varied activities.

Put the Bible up on a screen, or use a Bible app from stage when you are teaching rather than a hard copy.

Show kids they can have the Bible in every possible translation right in the palm of their hand. Yes, it's still the Bible!

Adjust your teaching. Make it active. Use stories. Keep them engaged!

14

Be Unpredictable: Engage Them with Variety

Predictable is boring!

Keep your kids on their toes. Don't allow your classes to become so predictable that your students know what to expect each week. Try some of the following ideas and surprise your class the next time they come.

Let Kids Hold the Remote

Kids love to be in control of things. Don't we all? But while they are children, there is very little they can control. Let them hold the remote control every now and again in your classes.

- Give your kids a voice by allowing them to choose the songs, games, or activities.
- Vote on ideas and include them in your planning.

- Develop a kid's focus group and ask them what they like and dislike and what they'd change.
- Ask them for some ideas for a new teaching series, or have them vote on options for the next set of lessons.
- Ask for their opinions for improving an event or program. Who is better to evaluate "kid content" than a kid?

If you give them a voice, maybe they'll listen!

Change It Up

While we would love to be able to improve our kid's short attention spans and focus, it's not a viable goal in our one hour a week. We need to work with the time we have.

With that in mind, try to use a variety of different activities to engage each of the different learning styles.

- Play games that relate to the lesson and have a purpose (don't play for the fun part and then make kids sit and be quiet for the Bible study).
- Move kids out of their chairs and involve them physically through energy-burning relays or other lively activities.

It isn't that they are trying to misbehave or be disobedient; God just wired them to move! An effective teacher channels that creative energy into learning experiences. Allow for something crazy now and then!

Years ago, our son loved his Sunday School teacher. Every week, he was blown away with a different creative teaching method that his teacher employed. One week he would bring in a model of something he had made, and then next he had something for the boys to make. He still remembers the time when Mr. M. set something on fire in the classroom and allowed one of the kids to use a fire extinguisher to put it out.

Now, that's not something I would necessarily recommend, but the point is that Mr. M. prepared well and taught well. And yes, occasionally he would do something crazy.

He would also regularly invite his class over to his home for fun activities. One time, he took the class to his house after a snowstorm, tethered together a stack of wood pieces, and dragged the boys around with his lawnmower through his yard. He fed them dinner, and they finished with a snowball fight and sledding. He knew how to build relationships with his kids.

It's great if you can do something different each week.

- Try meeting in a different room once in a while if that's a possibility.
- Meet outside when the weather permits.
- Create a casual atmosphere in your programs.
- Whenever you can, move your class to a location fitting for the topic, like a lakeshore for a study on Jesus' disciples.
- Look up creative ideas in other books and replace the not-so-exciting activities in your curriculum.
- Borrow a video camera or use your cell phone and capture a biblical drama to replay for kids. Have kids role-play a situation or act out the Bible stories as you read.
- Use creative writing and have kids write advice to Bible characters who are facing a big decision.

- Give kids the task of preparing a skit or an art project which presents the message of the passage.

Whatever you do, make your lessons unpredictable and different so that kids are always guessing what next week will include. The worst thing we can be for this generation is "predictable" or "boring".

Of course, these ideas are all very wonderful when you have well behaved kids, but what do you do when you have that one child who is able to wreak havoc on everything in less than sixty-seconds?

You know your class, and how much they can handle. Discretion is always the better part of valor. Use your judgment when teaching, but whenever possible, be creative and unpredictable.

Learn a New Language

Knowing that technology is here to stay is a strong indicator that it's time for us to accept it and even embrace its use in our classrooms. The need for Scripture in the teaching of today's youth hasn't changed, but the way they access and experience the story for themselves has.[102] We can doggedly remain committed to our flannel boards and puppets, but don't be surprised if you notice the kids staring off into space.

Now before you protest, I am not against flannel boards and puppets. But incorporate them into a variety of teaching methods, rather than using them every week.

For most of us, recent technological advances are a confusing, foreign world with which we would rather not have to interact. The thought of learning to interact with the ins and outs of confusing software, apps, downloads, uploads has you thinking, "It's all Greek to me!" You may say, "you can't teach an old dog new tricks" or "it's above my pay grade".

> However, the inevitable result of this new language that our kids are speaking is that if we want to reach them, we must have at least a rudimentary level of understanding.

For those of you who are terrified of Google Drive or who have no idea how to search the internet, take heart. Technology is constantly evolving and improving and much of it is fairly easy to use.

Learn everything you can about using computers in ministry. Ask a kid to teach you and use it as an opportunity to form relationships. Use the teen's technological skills to enhance your ministry and give them the opportunity to serve.

The kids in our classes will soon be rolling their eyes if we put a CD into a player or use a DVD. Out with the old, in with the new. We must keep learning, and if we claim to be lifelong learners, we must include technology in that process.

This new generation of kids prefers the interactivity of computer games, Internet, and video games. They won't be content as passive observers; they want to be involved.

Use a music/video countdown and sound effects when appropriate. There are a ton of inexpensive online games now available which are as simple as pressing "play". We need to ask ourselves some unfamiliar and perhaps uncomfortable questions like:

What does the Christian lifestyle look like in a digital world?

How can Alphas live out their Christian faith using technology?

How can we use technology to interface with the timeless Christian message?

As leaders, we need to ask these questions and listen to this generation for input and ideas.

It will be interesting to see what direction the curriculum

companies will go with this new "language". It's a whole new level of programing.

Interestingly, three out of four parents are not yet using any digital resources to help their child engage with the Bible even though some is now available.[103] Encourage them to search out the new apps and websites, and while you're doing so, check them out yourself!

- What if church became the place where kids were taught to use technology as a way to learn about their faith?
- What if we were able to teach discernment when it comes to the abundance of multi-media and advertising they see every day on their social media?
- What if the church could be on YouTube producing videos on relevant topics?
- What if, when a question was asked in class, we responded with, "Let's look it up together!"

Why not have children design an interactive computer game for the lesson?

Lead kids in creating a video re-enactment of Bible stories or producing their own music videos. Enlist older kids to make innovative commercials for your announcements.

Create a website, apps, or games to interact with the lesson.

Create a worship video together, take photos, and put pictures to words.

This might require enlisting some tech savvy people from your congregation, but it also might be a great way to engage some of the men who normally wouldn't step foot in a kid's classroom.

Technology can enhance our lessons; but the flipside, of course, is that we can become too dependent on it or distracted by it. Technology, no matter how advanced it becomes, will never replace the effectiveness of live teaching.

In an age when kids spend countless hours looking at screens from phones, tablets, computers, televisions, and game systems, we can make the mistake of over-utilizing this technology in our teaching. Technology has made our lessons more visual, made our ministries more secure, increased the speed of communication, and so much more. But we need to make sure that it is serving us. The balance is important.

15

Walt vs Fred: Magic or Reality?

When you compare the kingdoms of Walt and Fred, you will see two different ways in which they saw the world. Walt's "Disney World" was his perfect version of what our world should look like, whereas Fred's "Mr. Roger's Neighborhood" was simple, even plain.

Walt created a world that was an escape from the real world.

Fred lived in a neighborhood and showed kids how to navigate through the real world.[104]

Walt's world is a once-in-a-lifetime magical experience (or more often if your family has enough money) designed to entertain kids.

Church, on the other hand, is a regular event, and maintaining that Disney level of energy and creativity is not possible with the budget and schedule we keep.

There is nothing wrong about wanting church to be a fun event and an escape from the difficulties of the week, but it cannot be our first priority.

The "Fun" Debate

Ah, the "fun" question! How much fun is too much?

Yes, kids want to have fun.

They will either have fun under your direction, or they'll have fun at your expense.

> Have you ever noticed that when parents come to pick up their children, 9 times out of 10 you will hear them ask two questions? The first question they usually ask is, "Did you have fun?"

Yes, fun is important, but it should be a means to an end, not the goal. While having fun is essential, it should not come at the cost of substance. It's not the church's responsibility to compete with what the world is offering on this front, nor is it possible to do so. We need to find a balance between substance and engaging programming without spending too much time or energy on entertainment.

Barna discovered that "fun" was considered by most children's pastors to be the least important priority, yet these same leaders state that they meet this objective more effectively than any other. It is what they spend most of their time planning for and most of their budget paying for.

> . . . participants pointed the finger at themselves recognizing their priorities have gotten off-track. In their desire to be effective, sometimes children's ministry leaders have tried too hard to make their programming enjoyable and entertaining. Fun or style has unwittingly replaced substance and sometimes even sidelining the Gospel . . . there is a growing sense of resolve that something needs to change.[105]

The second question most parents will ask when they collect their children from your classroom will often be,

"What did you learn?"

Parents want to know that their kids enjoyed themselves, but they also hope that they learned something.

Was it engaging?

Was it relevant?

Do they want to come back?

So yes, fun is important, but it must be balanced with learning. How is your balance?

Another way to see God working is to involve the kids in serving. The Bible gives many examples of young people serving others.[106] Providing opportunities for children to serve not only helps the wellbeing of others; it is also key for their own wellbeing.

When children are anxious or depressed, serving can help to take the focus off themselves and put it onto somebody else. "It's not to minimize their pain, but to put it in perspective. Their own problems tend to fade into the background for a little while, while reaching out to somebody else."[107]

Today's kids belong to a generation that has an abundance of empathy for those who are less fortunate.

- Provide opportunities for them to help those in need.
- If you collect an offering, share with them the impact their giving is having.
- Teach them to care for one another and stand up for those who are being bullied.
- Expose them to genuine needs in the community and let them decide what to do about them.
- Inspire students with stories of leaders who have served.

Instead of awarding prizes for the kids, have them earn points which convert into helping a family in need. Convert their Bible bucks into groceries for a family. Work with the mission team to purchase chickens, goats, or water purifiers for missionaries in third world countries. Share reports and show pictures of their points at work. Add a giant world map and place pins where their points have helped. Kids can learn first-hand that it is "better to give than to receive."

Rather than going on a retreat, run a service camp where the students serve for a week in a needy city. During the day, they can work in the community, paint houses, do yardwork, pick up trash at the parks, serve lunch to those in need, or a host of other service projects. And then in the evenings, have something fun for them to do together.

Have you noticed when kids return from a missions or outreach trip, they exhibit a deeper spiritual commitment? Serving others helps kids begin to internalize and apply their faith as participants, not just spectators. When people engage in serving, they will be more consistent in their attendance. Kids don't have to wait until they are adults to serve. When we let kids be the church today, it helps activate their faith and makes it come alive!

> *Let no one despise your youth, but be an example to the believers in word, in conduct, in love, in spirit, in faith, in purity.* (1 Tim. 4:12)

Challenge your kids and allow them to see God at work in their lives. Instead of conditioning them to think that it's all about them, help them learn to intentionally love others.

Fun is important. Let's face it: if they don't have fun, they won't come back! And then it doesn't matter how active or varied your lessons are.

But fun is not the end game.

They also need to learn.

They need to learn to love God and others.

Fred's goal was different to Walt.

He didn't distract kids from the pain and questions that were making them sad or scared.

He looked in the camera and spoke from his heart to theirs.[108]

Kids don't need to be entertained as much as they need to love and be loved and thankfully, this task is possible.

We need to be Walt sometimes but Fred always.

Does your ministry need some reassessing? How is your teaching?

Knowing that Alphas learn more by experiencing and doing, involve them more, interact with them more.

Use stories and variety and creativity.

Give them a say in areas which warrant it and incorporate technology when you can.

Help them experience God and serve others.

And yes, have fun.

Please realize that this chapter has shared a multitude of ideas, projects, and methods. It was never intended for you to try to incorporate them all; that would be impossible.

The goal was to provide a kind of menu of options for you to think through and to help you become excited and hopeful about trying something new.

Perhaps choose one or two suggestions and implement them in your teaching.

Don't feel overwhelmed.

Just challenge yourself to step out of the box and try something different.

Don't forget, the most important thing is to love them and listen to them.

16

A Three-Cord Strand: Church, Family, and God

We've always known that parents are the ones to whom God has given the responsibility of child training. Any indication that we have circumvented that command has no doubt been unintentional. But according to the disheartening statistics we are hearing, our efforts to encourage and support our families are still falling short.

Families are struggling, and the church needs to come alongside for support.

A three-cord strand—the church working to support the family in their relationships with God—is the perfect team combination.

> *Though one may be overpowered by another, two can withstand him. And a threefold cord is not quickly broken.* (Eccl. 4:12)

We must strategize ways to draw families back in and allow the church to be a resource for meaningful biblical support. But how?

Celebrate Together

Milestones mark and celebrate life-changing moments in a family's spiritual journey. Key times include baby dedications, baptism, graduations, and transitions to new school grades. We need to take advantage of the opportunity that milestones provide us to reach the family.

You can use these moments to facilitate a special class designed to equip and encourage the parents, so they are ready for the next phase of their child's life. Each milestone is the perfect time for a celebration.

- Use the opportunity to involve the parents in a training class for each transition.
- Make a big deal of the festivities by providing invitations and refreshments.
- Designate a special table for each family to decorate and have a photographer on hand to take pictures.

Most extended family members, churched or unchurched, will happily attend a milestone celebration. The milestones can be wonderful shared experiences for the kids and their parents, as well as excellent outreach opportunities. One of my family members is not a believer, nor is he open to attending churches. But when our youngest child was baptized, she invited him and he came.

Parent & Child Dedication

There is nothing more exciting than the birth of a child, and you have an amazing opportunity to impact new parents who want to dedicate their baby to the Lord. This is the perfect chance to teach a class for the parents on biblical parenting and review their responsibility to raise their child in the faith. Maybe teach a class for the grandparents also since they have a responsibility, too.

- Plan a special service where you celebrate and commission each family.
- Present the family with a Dedication Certificate.
- Include a verse (chosen by the parents) and have them read the verse during the ceremony if possible.

Bible Presentation

When a child enters elementary school, provide a class to prepare the family and child to transition to the next level of learning. Children and parents can learn together about how we received the Bible and how to make it an important part of their life.

- Provide a Bible which can be used during elementary school.
- Have the parents present it to their child along with a special verse which they write it in the front.

Salvation

Most parents would love to be present when their child first trusts Jesus for the free gift of salvation. It doesn't always work that way, but we can still provide an opportunity to celebrate after the fact.

On an appropriate Sunday, invite parents to attend a "Salvation" class with their child, and use this as an opportunity to explain the gospel and what it means to trust Christ.

While we don't want to pressure them in any way, sharing the gospel in this format allows for further teaching and understanding. It will also provide the opportunity for parents to hear the gospel outlined in a simple and easy format.

Baptism

When a child indicates an interest in being baptized, provide a brief class for them and their parents to attend.

- Explain what baptism is, why you should be baptized, and when you should be baptized. Use the time to explain what will happen during the event in order to help alleviate any concerns.
- Help the child verbalize their faith, recording it in video form for the event.
- Again, provide invitations and refreshments.
- Have a photographer on hand to take pictures and give a copy to the family, along with a copy of the recorded testimony.

Graduation

One of the most important transitions for kids is the one from children's ministry to the student ministry. This is a key time to partner with your student ministry leader and work with them to make the transition as seamless as possible.

Preteens will be excited but insecure, so meeting together with the new leaders will help ease the nerves. Some kid's ministry leaders might even consider moving up with the preteens into the student ministry.

- Tie the event to a class that parents and their children attend together.
- Discuss how to parent a teenager and how to survive the teen years.
- Co-teach the class with your student ministry pastor/ director. This will help him or her connect with the family.
- Present each graduating child with a "teen" Bible.

One of my favorite gifts to give was a boomerang with the children's ministry logo on one side and the student ministry logo on the other. Included was an invitation for them to "return" as a future leader. We also presented them with a teen Bible, with a special verse from their parents. Again, provide invitations, refreshments, and a photographer.[109]

Serve Together

Some of the best activities for families to do together involve service opportunities. Some quick research will reveal the needs and opportunities in your local community where families could serve together. Possible suggestions might be serving at a homeless shelter, visiting shut-ins, or giving away bottles of water at community events.

One of our best attended family events was the annual assembling of shoeboxes for Operation Christmas Child each year. Pizza was provided after church, tables were set up around the building, and the donations collected throughout the year were divided and sorted. Children and parents alike assembled a shoebox and then selected items for each one. The children loved being able to pick out the perfect gifts for their box. It was the ideal event for families of any size or age.

Instead of planning a mission trip just for the youth, perhaps organize one where the older children could accompany their parents and serve together. Youth return home on fire spiritually after their experiences serving people in need in a different town or culture. Imagine the memories if mom and dad went on the mission trip with them.

Years ago, my husband took our son who was seven at the time to Nicaragua on a mission trip with our church. They have memories from that trip that will last a lifetime. The recollection of poorly dressed children crammed into a one-room house with dirt floors will forever be imprinted on our son's mind, a reminder of how rich we are in this country. Perhaps his tender heart for suffering people today began in that small Nicaraguan town.

> No matter how busy their schedules might be, families still crave events which will bring them together and create memories. The church can be a part of this.

Game nights, an intergenerational movie night followed by a lively discussion about the lesson it demonstrated, craft events where families build something, father-son campouts, mother-daughter tea events, daddy-daughter dances, family hiking event, family retreats, the list goes on.

Our favorite church event back in the days of our church plant was the annual family retreat. Most of our families would attend, and the weekend was designed to create memories together. Our kids would talk about the family game night on those retreats for months after we got home. Years later, they are still a treasured memory!

Worshipping Together?

There has been much discussion and debate over the years regarding whether or not it is beneficial to have children in the worship service with their parents, or whether they should have their own service. Some feel very strongly one way or the other.

But I wonder—does it have to be an either-or?

Many argue for one of the extremes as though our options are only "age-graded education" or "blended corporate worship".

Does it have to be an either/or issue, or can it be a both/and?

Are there ways that we could creatively gather kids and parents into shared experiences?

Honestly, both extremes have their difficulties.

Historically, families have worshipped together. Author Ivy Beckwith says, "In Scripture, the passing on of faith was always done intergenerationally, informally and formally. The idea of generations isolated from each other was unheard of."[110]

Scripture also seems to suggest that children met with adults in the worship gatherings. Letters were read aloud to the assembly, and in each letter some words are addressed directly to the children.

Keeping children in church allows them the chance to observe their parents' faith and worship within the tradition of their church as well as experience the church ordinances of baptism and communion. It can also serve as a reminder to the congregation; instead of just focusing on the present needs, they can see the next generation and remember to include and pray for them.

We could involve the children in a variety of ways, from the announcements (direct to children; announce children's programs; greet the children separately) to worship (include something upbeat for the children; involve them in worship band; explain words in song).

The prayer time might include requests from children or

birthdays that take place that week. There could be reserved seating for families where kids can see what's going on, children's worship resources, and service opportunities allowing children to help by welcoming people, handing out bulletins, collecting the offering, reading Scripture, or serving communion together with their family.

This might enable children to feel a part of the whole church instead of being hidden in the forgotten back corners of the church.

> . . . A faith community that facilitates the positive spiritual formation of its members is one where the generations know and respect each other—not one where the generations are separated from each other, with no significant relationships between them . . . so why has it been so difficult to convince people of the importance of mixing the generations together? [111]

One thing is for sure: if we are going to integrate children into the adult worship service of the church, we must cater for them and have the pastor's full support. Choosing to include the children in corporate worship will bring with it some accompanying complications, namely increased seating requirements and the inevitable distractions, especially for the parents who spend most of their time either entertaining them or trying to keep them quiet.

> The predominant mind-set in Christian education concerning families has long been that "to strengthen the whole, you must strengthen the parts." That's why at church, we deliver Christian education, and often worship, in age groups . . . . But families need more from church life than age-graded programs and the occasional all-church

> activity . . . Many of our church activities actually draw family members apart from each other. We know something is wrong with this picture, but sorting out a solution seems complicated.[112]

To help with this, a church could possibly provide a class that gives instruction and suggestions for these families, including the importance of worship and the preference to arrive early for the necessary bathroom trips and seating. Children could be taught how to use the hymn book, what to do when they have a need or question, and why it's important to be respectful (not interrupting, changing seats, taking seconds of communion, etc.).

On the other side of the debate, we live in a very age-stratified culture. "The church has just followed suit, creating segments of ministry that appeal to certain age groups as a way of attracting them . . . "[113] And . . . it might be easier than trying to solve the issues that arise from keeping everyone together.

Think about it.

Unfortunately, in our current culture, the generations do not respect each other any longer! With the breakdown of society and disintegration of family structures, the reality of family worship has become increasingly difficult if not impossible. It's hard to have family worship when there is no "family unit."

We also need to remember that the biblical command is to teach children. Whatever method our community and church culture will allow, that is our responsibility. Teach the next generation.

And while a legitimate argument could be made for children learning from the sermon, it's a fact that children will not fully understand adult teaching and learn like they will in a class designed especially for them (which has the added benefit of giving their parents a break and providing more seating).

We can find ways to include the children when we can.

- When we know that a baptism is taking place, we can spend time during the children's lesson talking about baptism, and then bring the oldest classrooms into the main worship so they can observe.
- If there is a baby dedication, we can bring the kids in to watch.
- We can teach the older classes about communion and have them observe the service.

Leadership requires finding and developing that balance in your individual church setting.

Families are looking for opportunities to make spiritual memories, so let's not disappoint them.

We can celebrate together, incorporating a time of learning and festivities as children reach each milestone.

We can find ways that families can serve together, helping to teach their children to be less self-centered while at the same time, providing for them to spend time with their parents.

And we can think through ways to worship together, finding a way to creatively bring children and parents into shared experiences.

Let's be the third strand in the cord so it is not easily broken.

Let's find ways to work together with our families to help them in their walk with God. They are trying to call their children in, away from the distractions of the world, but they need our voice to help.

17

Call a Friend? Be a Lifeline for Millennial Parents

Every parent needs a friend. Someone who they can call on when they feel overwhelmed, fearful, frustrated, or not sure how to handle the issues that their children are facing. In the last chapter, we talked about how we might be able to incorporate families into the church, but we also have a responsibility to equip, encourage, and engage the parents as they deal with the huge challenge of parenting in today's world.

Earn Their Trust

Before we can help parents, we must first earn their trust.

When our children were small, my husband was very reticent to leave them with anybody, known or unknown. With the stories of abuse becoming common place, his trust levels were extremely low.

The first time we left our oldest daughter, Hannah, was during a Christian retreat weekend. They offered childcare, and we went to check it out. There was a notice on the wall that each of the workers had been screened and background checked, which was our number one concern. As we looked around, everything seemed well organized and clean. The young lady approached us with a big smile and was very friendly and reassuring. We were still tentative, but we had no other choice.

We returned an hour later to check, and our daughter was alive and well.

On another occasion, we were vacationing near the Great Smokey Mountains when we visited a large church and again faced the same issue. My husband wanted to keep our daughter with us, but she was excited to go and play with the other kids. I encouraged him to at least check it out, and we were greeted by two lovely ladies who immediately put him at ease and reassured him. The room was clean and organized, they had a security system in place, and we were given an individualized tag that was required for pick up. Hannah ran off happily to play and we returned to the service.

With all the scandals, abuse, accusations, lack of accountability, and hypocrisy, many parents are cautious about trusting businesses, churches, and organizations with their children.

> Our role as ministry leaders is to first build trust with the parents. That takes time and intentionality, but it is key if you want to reach today's kids by impacting their parents.

We've known for some time that security systems are essential for our children's ministry. Child-security is a fundamental requirement for any organization that works with minors. In fact, most insurance companies require some sort of child safety policies to be in place whenever children are involved.

Churches must take measures to ensure the children are safe and secure. Volunteers must be screened and trained so that a hedge of protection surrounds our children and our church. Parents are entrusting us with the spiritual and physical responsibility of children, and we must meet that challenge head on.

The obvious measures include enforcing a six-month attendance rule for new volunteers before they can serve with children, screening all volunteers with a written application, background and reference checks, and a personal interview and training.

But are there additional measures needed for this technologically advanced generation? What new issues will we face? Sexual predators, domestic violence, custody issues, and restraining orders have been with us for years, but technology has further complicated them and multiplied the dangers. We need to be prepared for anything.

Last summer, we were in the middle of our week-long annual fun camp when we noticed an unfamiliar car entering our parking lot. Immediately behind it came a police vehicle, followed a minute later by two more police cars. A scuffle followed as the police attempted to wrestle the female suspect from the car. She was very scantily dressed, and body areas were more visible than they should have been to anyone observing. It took some time, but the police were finally able to handcuff her and place her in the police car.

The children were thankfully in the middle of snack time inside, but of course the episode was visible from the window and word traveled. Half of the kids were scheduled to head outside in a few minutes, but our trained volunteers wisely improvised, adjusted the schedule (so that everyone remained behind the now-locked doors), and closed the curtains. We immediately emailed the parents, knowing that the news would travel quickly, and it would be preferable for them to hear the story without any embellishments from us. The whole event lasted several hours before the police drove away, but thankfully no harm was done. It was, in the end, a great opportunity for our leaders to see the value in our security training.

Situations happen, often without notice. While we had not specifically trained for that particular incident, our leaders knew enough to act appropriately, and the parents were very grateful for their actions. While we can't prepare for every possible scenario, our responsibility is to do what we can.

> Courts have generally held that no organization can be expected to protect its children from bizarre or completely unforeseen types of harm. In the event of a lawsuit, courts usually ask some variation of the question: Did the organization take reasonable and prudent precautions to protect the child?[114]

Having said that, we must schedule regular training for our team, both for security and for safety.

Train your team about the importance of appropriate touch (side hugs, high-fives, fist bumps, pats on the back), and never using any physical discipline when correcting children (even their own child as observers may not know who they are).

Explain the necessity of preventing unapproved adults from entering a classroom and the use of a secure check-in and check-out system to ensure that children are released only to an authorized person. Of course, the most critical requirement to teach our teams is that two unrelated adults must be always present in a classroom, no exceptions.

Ensure Their Safety

Unfortunately, injuries do happen. Ask yourself, "Does this look safe?" We need to do everything in our power to ensure the safety of their children.

- Make sure that your playgrounds use modern equipment safety standards with regular maintenance and that they are well fenced.
- Inform parents of any injury, large or small. Parents are usually understanding and appreciative when we are upfront about accidents.
- Have an emergency plan in place to answer questions such as what to do regarding fire alarms, active shooters, or lockdowns.
- Train your leaders to know what to do when there is an issue.
- Enlist a security team of well-trained people.

Thinking these questions through ahead of time and training your volunteers will prevent chaos in the event of an emergency.

Returning to the story about our daughter's experience in the preschool room, we spent the beginning of the service wondering if she was happy and safe when our phone vibrated. The preschool teacher had texted us a photo of Hannah smiling and playing with the other children. She was safe and happy, so as parents we relaxed. It was a great way to reassure new parents, and we incorporated the same idea in our ministry years later.

The Millennial generation doesn't trust institutions. They have seen the financial discrepancies that sometimes creep into the church. They have read about the moral failures of leaders. They have heard about the accusations of abuse.

Let's make sure that our children's ministry reflects a love for their kids and is being handled with excellence. Perhaps then we can earn their trust again!

Equip Them with Resources

When it comes to parents, most feel ill-equipped and untrained for successful parenting. How can we help them?

Only one in five church leaders say they prioritize training for parents, and even fewer provide parenting guides or other resources.[115] Most parents say they are interested in parenting resources that address their specific circumstances or their child's life stages but often don't know how or where to find biblically-sound resources. It might be as simple as creating lists of helpful books, websites, articles, and podcasts, and then making them available.

Parents need help.

They are hungry for answers and willing to learn from each other.

What if we offered monthly parenting seminars on different topics? We could feed and spend time with their kids, the parents could enjoy a night off without needing to hire a babysitter, and as an added bonus, learn a new skill. It could be the perfect time to talk about those sensitive cultural issues like gender identity, childhood trauma, technology, self-harm, and suicide. These classes could be taught by someone from your church or community, or by using a video teaching series.

Offer classes on basic Christian life topics like salvation and assurance, how to have a daily walk with God, Bible study and memorization, sin and tempation, prioritizing time and finances, etc. Parents cannot be expected to disciple their children if they don't understand. If you provide quality, relevant, and Bible-based teaching, most parents will welcome it.

Prepare parents in advance with the tools they need to answer the hard questions that will inevitably come. Encourage them to take the initiative and address the issues before they impact their family.

Form "focus groups" to connect parents who have children of the same ages and provide an opportunity for them to talk. You could take a similar approach with the kids, providing food and addressing a topic that is relevant to where they are. Another possibility might be an online parenting forum on social media allowing them share tips and tools for discipling their kids, marriage advice, or articles about parenting.

Explore ways to encourage parents to continue the conversation with their kids at home. One issue that church leaders are seeing is that kids are not integrating what they learned on Sundays into their everyday life.

- What if we recorded the Sunday lessons and sent it out each week?
- Encourage families to turn off their devices during meals and provide "Table Talkers"[116] for them to use, an excellent resource with conversation starters, jokes, and activities.
- Create a Spotify playlist with our memory verse songs and encourage them to play it in the car while driving from activity to activity. This redeems otherwise dead time and maybe the parents will also learn a verse or two along the way.
- Organize an event where the whole family can attend, have dinner, and then participate in a devotional time together. While most parents would agree that family devotionals can be effective, many of them do not know where to find quality material.
- Demonstrate how to pray together, read the Bible, listen to worship music, and have a spiritual discussion.
- Send family devotionals via email for them to use.

Encourage Them with Mentors

Relationships are a big deal to millennials. Many recognize the need for advice and would love for someone who will walk through the tough parts of life with them. Mentoring is the perfect solution, either in a formal or informal capacity. It is an opportunity to receive a different perspective, be held accountable, and to share helpful, biblical advice.

Mentoring is a relationship between two people: a bridge between generations, and a tool for spiritual, mental, emotional, and physical growth. Mentorship is doing life together, sharing meals, enjoying common activities, and so much more.

> *Therefore encourage one another and build each other up, just as in fact you are doing.* (1 Thess. 5:11 NIV)

When I was a relatively young mom, I was juggling my parenting responsibilities as well as those of being a pastor's wife. Not an easy task. I had been praying for and searching for an older lady who might invest a little of her time and life experience to mentor me.

One of the most difficult things I ever did was ask, "Would you be my mentor?" Talk about feeling vulnerable!

What if she said "no" or didn't want to?

The flip side is also difficult. A number of years later, I was the older mom and had the desire to invest myself in a younger mom. I felt that same vulnerability as I asked her if she wanted my friendship.

I am not sure how to avoid those fears. It just required me to take a chance and ask. Both times the reply was "yes" and it was well worth it. I know that many people would never ask, and the ideal is to let a friendship naturally evolve, but the reality is that this rarely happens.

At the very least, we can begin to pray for someone to encourage. Be on the lookout for someone who could use a friend. We all need help and encouragement. We could all use a mentor.

Engage Them with Technology

Millennials are the parents you are trying to communicate with and they are known for being current with technology. Most millennials want to use social media to influence others. Realize that:

Ninety-five percent of Millennial moms have a smart phone.[117]

Ninety-eight percent of text messages are read within 3 minutes or less.[118]

Eighty-nine percent use Instagram.[119]

They post and read often. We can use social media to engage them.

- Instead of asking them to visit your website, go to them.
- Learn how to use Facebook, Snap Chat, Twitter, Instagram, Pinterest, or whatever app is most common in your community.
- Use it to promote upcoming events, series, and programs.
- Ask parents to help share the posts.

Parents also love photos and videos of their children. In fact, 98 percent of them will post pictures on social media of their experiences.[120]

- If you have a family event at church, post pictures rather than typing up what happened (always have permission before posting photos of children).

- Provide photo opportunities at church where Millennial parents can use their smartphones to take pictures with their kids. You can be sure the moms will post them online.
- Use your phone to create short online videos to post online.
- Provide social media posts about the ministry that parents can share online and use to invite their friends to church.

We purchased an inexpensive photo booth backdrop and on special occasions and outreaches (Easter, Fall, Christmas), we would set it up with colorful seasonal backgrounds. We provided a photographer who took family photos, and the parents loved it. It didn't take much effort or cost, but it was a great way to connect with visiting families.

- Create a closed Facebook group for parents only, to share lessons, take home papers, weekly photos of classes, volunteers, and pertinent topics for discussion. Millennial parents are looking for activities to do with their children so include activities that parents can do with their children that tie into the lesson of the week.
- Provide updates, a recap of the lesson, parenting tips, and short devotionals for kids and parents to do together.

Millennials want to be part of shaping the future of the church so give them opportunities to do so. Families want the ability to help shape the future of the churches that we are asking them to attend and participate in, so allow them a voice.

Ask them what they would change in the church if they were given the opportunity.

Earn their trust.

Equip them with resources.

Ensure their safety.

Encourage them with mentors.

Engage them with technology.

Let's support them in their critical task of parenting.

They are watching while their children are playing in the dark.

They are on the frontlines.

The fireflies are glowing.

Help parents be the voice to call them in before it's too late.

18

The Untapped Resource: Activating Men

Are you struggling for volunteers?

I'm here to tell you that everyone else is struggling, too. It's supposedly the most challenging aspect of children's ministry—finding good leaders. But what if we have neglected an important potential volunteer group in the church?

Men!

Now I know this may have your brain spinning already. Men in children's ministry? Get a grip! They'll never do it.

I beg to differ. Keep an open mind, and let's take a plunge into that undiscovered resource.

Children's Ministry Is Very "Pink"

Have you noticed how pink it is in children's ministry? A huge imbalance between men and women exists in most of the church's volunteer teams, and the disparity in children's ministry is even greater.

The subtle message that men hear is that children's ministry is for women. But Scripture sends a clear message that we need a gender balance. Females provide the gentle care and nurture, but men balance that with encouragement, urging, and challenging.

As a mother ***comforts*** *her child, so will I comfort you . . .* (Isa. 66:13 NIV; emphasis mine)

Just as a nursing mother ***cares*** *for her children, so we cared for you. Because we loved you so much . . .* (1 Thess. 2:7-8 NIV; emphasis mine)

For you know that we dealt with each of you as a father deals with his own children, ***encouraging, comforting*** *and* ***urging*** *you to live lives worthy of God . . .* (1 Thess. 2:11-12 NIV; emphasis mine)

Women are designed to comfort and care, but men are built to encourage and urge. We have different strengths and we need both. Fathers are charged with the role of disciplining their children and are to raise their children in the training and admonition of the Lord.

. . . For whom the Lord loves He disciplines, Just as a father ***disciplines*** *the son in whom he delights.* (Prov. 3:12 NASB; emphasis mine)

. . . For what children are not ***disciplined*** *by their father?* (Heb. 12:7 NIV; emphasis mine)

And you, fathers, do not provoke your children to wrath, but bring them up in the ***training*** *and* ***admonition*** *of the Lord.* (Eph. 6:4; emphasis mine)

"Admonition" carries with it the idea of steering a boat course, with corrections when necessary, and "nurture" means gentle instruction. Both discipline and admonition are needed in our kid's classes, but often the responsibility for dealing with them is left to the ladies.

> Sociologists tell us that mothers tend to emphasize the emotional security of their children, while fathers tend to stress competition and risk taking. Mothers also tend to seek the immediate wellbeing of the child, while fathers tend to foster long-term autonomy and independence. Children of both sexes appear to learn self-control and responsibility primarily from their fathers.[121]

Men can help teach competition and risk-taking, autonomy, self-control, and independence. These are all essential qualities for kids today. How many men do you have in your leadership team? Perhaps we should do a little strategizing to see if we can get them involved.

The Reasons They Say "No"

How do men feel about church? David Murrow's great book *Why Men Hate Going to Church* is instructive here. He makes some extremely good points related to how men feel when it comes to volunteering at church.

> Generally speaking, men's gifts and abilities do not match the ministry needs of the typical American congregation. Men are square pegs, trying to fit into a sea of round holes . . .
>
> You may be thinking. *What do you mean round holes? Men are welcome to every one of those positions!* It's not a question

> of welcome, but of expertise . . . Men want to serve in an area where they have experience and skill . . .
>
> Because men don't usually possess the soft skills needed for spiritual work, they tend to gravitate toward practical ministries: building, finance, usher, and committee work. But these square holes are not the core work of the church and may even be regarded as necessary evils that are less important than the round holes.[122]

Later in his book, he adds:

> Very few churches offer ministry opportunities that capitalize on men's skills and experience. Men long to give of their best to the Master, but few churches want what men have got.[123]

Barna found agreement after interviewing a nominal [male] churchgoer:

> When you reject the things I stand for—excellence, strategic thinking, progress, efficiency, vision, controlled risks, bottom-line performance—you reject me. I used to take it personally, but I've minimized the anger by making my church involvement less of a priority.[124]

If that is accurate, it explains the "pink" waves in children's ministry. Men don't feel that there is a place for them.

In fact, the opposite is the case. Our children's ministry needs men!

With the enormous percentage of families helmed by single mother and distant fathers, our kids need male influence in their lives. Without them, there will be many boys missing out on godly male role models.

But how do we attract them?

Men respond to needs if they are aware of them. It's in their nature to want to protect and provide where they are able. Making men aware of the need and urgency of child evangelism, as well as the influence they can have by challenging these kids and being a godly role model, will go a long way towards drawing them in.

> If you want to capture the heart of a man—especially a younger man—you have to offer him a shot at greatness. Men will not invest themselves wholeheartedly in any endeavor that does not offer this possibility.[125]

Men need to understand that the statistical 4-14 window of time is critical for children, and they can play a valuable part of reaching kids for Christ.

What is the 4-14 window? It is referring to the focus of evangelizing children between the ages of 4 and 14 years old when the receptivity is the greatest.

Men respond to challenges, and this is a challenge! Reach them before it's too late. They will often respond when they are challenged to do something which is achievable.

Men need to know that we need them!

Here's a message from a man who worked in our children's ministry:

> I work in children's ministry because of the joy and blessings that come from working with the kids. The joy of seeing them come to a saving faith in Jesus, or grow in their walk with God, and the blessings of seeing them have that "aha" moment.
>
> I would tell other men how important it is for us to be involved in children's ministry—some of the kids that come

to the church need a good, Christian, male role model. If we aren't there to fill that responsibility, who will?[126]

Adjust the Perception

Not only is children's ministry pink, the perception of it is also pink. We can adjust this quite simply.

- We could create environments that have less flowers and bunnies.
- We could stop talking about "parenting" and talk about "mothering" and "fathering".
- We could change the perception of kid's ministry by adjusting the wording on some of our policies and developing a more balanced vision.

For example, instead of "Children's Ministry: where your child will be safe, loved and nurtured," we could add, "and where your child will feel challenged and empowered."

Instead of saying, "Men are not permitted to change diapers" (which most wouldn't want to anyway), state, "Two adults must be present whenever a diaper is changed."

In our desperation to prevent a predator any access to our children, we may have inadvertently deterred men from assisting in a ministry which desperately needs their involvement and contribution.

Clearly explain the procedures.

Help them to understand what is expected of them. It is easy for men to feel untrusted and opt out of serving all together.

Triumphing over opposition, achieving a goal or winning a competition all lead to feeling great. What does triumph, achievement or winning look like in your children's ministry?[127]

Instead, why not develop roles specifically for men around their personality, gifts, and talents? Explain the challenge and allow them the chance to rise to the occasion. Present the reality of spiritual opposition and share how much they are needed. Allow them to see the goal and give them the opportunity to reach it.

Invite men to serve in entry level positions created especially for them to fill. You might find them willing to be the game leader, or in charge of technology, security, or events. Introduce activities that men enjoy.

Instead of just doing "crafts," let the men instruct the kids on how to build or create something. Ask the question, "What areas are men truly gifted in?" Let men know that their contribution to children's ministry is something unique to them, a need only they can fill.

Give them a specific job to do so that they don't feel out of place.

My husband would often serve as the second adult in a room when volunteers were lacking, but he didn't know what to do so he just sat on the sidelines. While he was doing me a favor, he felt like he was really not needed.

Men are "likely more at ease, more comfortable, more enthusiastic, more themselves, when doing an activity."[128]

It might have been better if I had said, "Would you be willing to sit in on this class which already has a teacher and just get to know the kids?"

Don't throw men in the deep end.

Wait for them to feel comfortable before increasing their responsibilities. Men enjoy serving alongside other men where they have each other's back.

Recruit them in pairs and allow them to lead activities together with a buddy.

Don't force them to feel isolated, serving only with another "pink" person.

When I think of men volunteering for service, I think of the military. Men will readily volunteer to give their lives in service for our country but the thought of volunteering to serve with children is the furthest thing from their minds.

I ask myself, "Why?" and wonder what we could do to attract more men.

Looking at the military websites, you find pictures of men (and women), lots of them, dressed smartly in uniform with the headline, "Learn about the benefits of serving your country, military career paths, and more."

> Joining the military can be an exciting and life-changing experience. There are a lot of reasons young men and women across the United States show an interest in the Armed Forces. Some have a multigenerational respect for the military and want to serve like their older relatives did. Others want job security and the benefits that come along with being in the military. Whatever the reason, joining the military can create a great foundation for future personal growth.[129]

Exciting and life-changing?

Job security and benefits?

Great foundation for future personal growth?

Rewards that will last far beyond this life?

Giving your life in service for the King of Kings?

Doesn't that sound just like children's ministry? Let's give men a chance to make a difference.

The untapped resource—men.

Let's find a way to invite and incorporate them into our kid's ministry that not only encourages them but also helps to reach our children.

Their voices are essential as we strive together to warn our children of the ever-increasing darkness which threatens to engulf them.

We need them to join in the chorus.

"When you see fireflies . . . "

Let's all call together.

PART FOUR

HOPE: Call Them In

Fireflies come from the same family as glowworms. Glowworms also light up, but the wings of the fireflies distinguish them from other luminescent insects. Their light is thought to also serve as a defense mechanism, flashing a clear warning of their unappetizing taste, a cautionary signal to predators. That didn't stop our children, however, as another of their favorite activities growing up was to try to catch a firefly in a jar. Occasionally, they were successful and were able to see these unique creatures up close, still glowing, on, off, on, off. Don't worry, they always released them back to their habitat.

Did you know that the average life span of a firefly is only about 2 months? Fireflies only glow for a short time, and then the sky returns to blackness. If we wanted to enjoy them, we needed to hurry. Their short life reflected the urgency of time before their glow would dim. In the same way, we have only a short window of time to reach the children in our communities before their receptiveness lessens.

This time is precious. Let's not waste it. There is still hope.

Call them in!

19

The Gospel Priority: The Need for Urgency

Be sober, be vigilant; because your adversary the devil walks about like a roaring lion, seeking whom he may devour. (1 Pet. 5:8)

Satan's goal is to steal, kill, and destroy (John 10:10). His priority is deception, and he is in the business of stealing sheep. He will do whatever it takes to prevent the lost from trusting in Jesus as their Savior.

It is so easy for other things to get in the way of our primary goal. The "urgent" crowds out the "important." The enemy loves it when distractions cause us to lose our focus. A common sentiment is expressed below:

> The desire to lead kids to Christ and disciple them is still the purpose that burns in the hearts of those who love the Lord and want to bring children to Him . . . But . . . we may have drifted from our purpose . . . Many fear that in

> the overwhelming busyness of running a children's ministry program, we may have lost sight of the priority.[130]
>
> . . . The gospel is the goal—not good programming, exciting events, or large numbers . . . So often as leaders we can become so involved in 'doing' ministry, we can forget about what ministry is all about—the Gospel.[131]

Whatever it takes!

This time in the life of a child is the most receptive they will likely ever be.

Let's be ready to hit a home run and put a dart in the center of the bull's eye.

Be Ready

The opportunity to share the gospel can come at any age or stage. Some might think that children are not capable of fully understanding all of the implications of the gospel message so we should wait until they're older to share the good news. But there are many stories of people who trusted in Jesus for salvation at the age of three or four.

Will a young child understand all of the implications of the gospel then? Of course not. I don't know about you, but I am still working to understand all of the implications of the gospel message, and I'm definitely still learning to allow Him to be the Lord of my life. But kids can understand the simple gospel message and Jesus' love.

If we were to wait until they fully understood everything, the right time might never come. Jesus made a point of telling us that kids are capable of trusting Him.

> *Let the little children come to me, and do not hinder them,* ***for the kingdom of heaven belongs to such as these.*** (Matt. 19:14 NIV; emphasis mine)

That verse alone should show us that simple, childlike faith is all that is required. Who are we to hinder these children?

Be Prepared

The ultimate goal and delight for any children's leader is the opportunity to lead a child to Christ! We should be always watching and praying for opportunities, ever mindful of the enormous responsibility we have as God's representatives.

How well prepared are you when the moment comes?

Many teachers fear that they'll say the wrong thing. The children we minister to are all at different ages, education and developmental levels, with various family and life experiences. Look at what Spurgeon says about sharing the gospel:

> Have a care what you are after when you pretend to be teaching them for God. Wound the child's hand if you will; but, for God's sake, do not wound his heart. Say what you like about temporal things; but I beseech you, in spiritual matters, take care how you lead him.[132]

In an effort to be consistent with our message, we incorporated "How to Share the Gospel" into our annual volunteer training and encouraged our volunteers to share the gospel often. They all memorized a simple outline and we used that same message in each class, adjusting the terminology to allow for age differences.

Bad News vs. Good News:

1. We are all sinners (Romans 3:23).
2. We all deserve death (separation from God) (Romans 6:23).
3. Jesus died to take our place (Romans 5:8).

4. God promises us eternal life if we believe (trust) in Him (John 3:16).

A very simple outline—four points and four verses.[133]

> We hung posters with this outline in every room. From Nursery to Preteen, kids heard the same four points, over and over. Rather than each teacher explaining it a different way, our hope was that the consistent message from year to year would stick with them.

We also taught our volunteers to use their own testimony as another effective way to share. Children love stories, and what better story for us to tell than our own.

It's possible to clearly present the gospel in only three or four sentences! Before we trusted in Jesus, how we trusted in Him, and after He saved us.[134] For example:

> When I was a kid, I went to Sunday school every week and I learned from the Bible that God loves me. But He is perfect, and I needed Jesus to save me from my sin (all the wrong things I had done). I learned that Jesus died on the cross in my place, and if I believed in Him, He promised to forgive me. Now I know I am part of His family and one day I will go to be with Him in heaven.

Encourage your volunteers to become comfortable sharing their story and to be prepared at any moment to be used by God.

Reassure the Unsure

Stories are plentiful of adults (including myself) who, as a young child, prayed to trust Christ repeatedly, just to make sure they were really saved.

A well-known children's ministry recently celebrated an event by posting on Facebook, "Forty-seven kids filled out salvation cards last night, with five being the first time."[135] Seemingly, forty-two children had previously indicated they were saved, but had again "filled out a card."

What is causing children to feel that they need to fill out another salvation card?

Peer pressure or a desire to please?

Did they fill out a card because their friend did?

Or were they confused about the message of salvation and lacking assurance?

Maybe it's all the above. One author writes:

> . . . don't discount a child's desire to pray for salvation on more than one occasion . . . my understanding of this commitment grew each year, which is why I kept praying . . . I just wanted **to be sure**" [emphasis added] . . . I don't find any passage in the Bible that says someone is wrong to pray a salvation prayer more than once. Although once is literally enough for eternity, praying more frequently might offer a child **greater comfort and certainty** [emphasis added].[136]

Rather than seeing this need for repetition as a source of comfort, it could stem from a place of uncertainty and fear.

> My repeated prayers for salvation were the result of a lack of assurance. I needed to be sure, so I prayed again. I was afraid of missing out on heaven, so I asked again.

That is not a position I would wish on any child.

Surely it would have been preferable to be sure from the beginning.

Lingering doubts about our eternity are no more helpful than a child who wonders if he will be thrown out of the family because of something that he did. If our kids are doubting their salvation, we need to help.

The feeling that we need to keep asking suggests that we are concerned because of something we have done.

"I hit my sister."

"I told a lie."

"Will I still go to heaven?"

The focus is on my sin.

But when we believe, we are believing that Jesus paid our sin penalty in full. Our sin has been completely taken care of—past, present, and future. There should be no doubt.

> The need to keep praying for salvation is actually an indication that we are looking within to ourselves, not at what Jesus has done for us.
> To be sure of our salvation, we must continue to look to Jesus, where we looked in the first place. He paid for our sin then, and it is still paid for now.

It's natural for kids to question. As they grow in their understanding (and their sin), questions can enter their minds. We need to find ways to reassure them. Our daughter worked as a camp counselor one summer where the staff introduced their own "Book of Life."

And I saw the dead, great and small, standing before the throne, and books were opened. Another book was opened, which is the

> *book of life. The dead were judged according to what they had done as recorded in the books . . . . Anyone whose name was not found written in the book of life was thrown into the lake of fire.* (Rev. 20:12,15 NIV)

Whenever a child trusts in Christ for salvation, they would add their name to the book, along with the date, as a commemoration of the event. At the end of the week, the camp would celebrate those lives. What a great idea.

If ever they doubt, they just need to remember their special day.

Some give "Faith Certificates" with the child's name and the date for them to hang in their bedroom as a reminder.

However you choose to help children commemorate the occasion, mark it by something special which will make it memorable, and if possible have them share it with their parents.

Reassure the unsure.

Deep or Wide?

Twenty-four percent of Generation Z kids say our teaching is shallow![137]

Is it possible that we are teaching to the lowest common denominator?[138]

It's true that not all kids have the same ability or knowledge, but they are capable often of more than we realize. Don't be guilty of "dumbing" down the Bible. Make sure that your kids know the basics and teach them thoroughly and well.

> We are raising a generation of children who are biblically illiterate . . . We are feeding them shallow, watered-down lessons that are not providing them with a faith foundation.[139]

Fluff, shallow, no solid biblical teaching? No sin, virtue-based teaching? Deconstruction movement? Progressive Christianity? Removing the cross from the gospel? Hopefully none of these phrases ring a bell in terms of your ministry.

Hudson tells a story about a class he was once teaching:

> Recently, I was serving in a children's ministry elementary classroom. I was sharing the gospel with the kids. I referenced John 3:16 and asked if someone would quote it for us. Out of a group of 20 kids, I was sure many of them knew John 3:16 . . . Not one child knew John 3:16. Even when I gave them a hint of the first few words of the verse . . . To be honest, this scared me. And for good reason. These are kids who have been raised in church. And they don't even know the basics of Biblical truth.[140]

How are your kids doing?

Are they biblically illiterate?

What are you feeding them?

There is a plethora of resources available out there, so if you need to reassess what you are teaching, there is no lack of options. Just remember, choosing "flash" over "foundation" is never an acceptable trade.

Make sure your curriculum is Bible-based and focuses on helping kids know God's Word and its key truths. Don't let them leave your class biblically illiterate.

Be on Guard

If children's ministry has the potential to lead the most people to Christ, then it follows that our enemy's strategy would be that we don't share the gospel or that we don't share it clearly! What better way to diffuse our ministry by distracting us from the real purpose or confusing the gospel message itself?

You are not sowing, as some say, on virgin soil, for it has long been occupied by the devil; but you are sowing on a soil more fertile now than it ever will be again, soil that will produce fruit now, far better than it will do in after days; you are sowing on a young heart, and what you sow will be pretty sure to abide there, especially if you teach evil, for that will never be forgotten.[141]

The Bible predicts that false teaching will be rampant in the last days.

> *For the time will come when they will not endure sound doctrine, but according to their own desires, because they have itching ears, they will heap up for themselves teachers; and they will turn their ears away from the truth, and be turned aside to fables.* (2 Tim. 4:3-4)

What would be the worst kind of "false teaching"? I think it's making a simple gospel message confused and unclear. We must guard our flock, maintain our true priority, and do not allow peripheral matters to distract us from our primary purpose.

> *Keep watch over yourselves and all the flock of which the Holy Spirit has made you overseers. Be shepherds of the church of God, which he bought with his own blood.*
>
> *I know that after I leave, savage wolves will come in among you and will not spare the flock. Even from your own number men will arise and distort the truth*
>
> *In order to draw away disciples after them.* (Acts 20:28-30 NIV)

Let me say to all of you who are children's leaders: a battle is raging . . . there is war for the souls of our children. Yes, we know who will ultimately win, but we have a huge part to play in the battle.

> It makes sense that if the 4-14 years are critical, the best antagonist would target these years in particular for distraction and destruction.

And Satan is the best deceiver out there, and he has no greater desire than to see our ministry to children become ineffective!

> . . . I believe the battlefront is found in the minds, hearts and souls of our children. Imagine yourself as Satan . . . what easier way to inflict the maximum possible pain upon God than by winning over His beloved creatures from the earliest possible moment, resulting in a lifetime of unrighteous behavior by those creatures? Win them early, and the job is all but finished.[142]

Satan knows that if he can destroy children, he can rule the world.

What better way to do that than by inoculating our children to the gospel? We should expect that this will be a priority for him.

Advertisers desire to influence everyone. Humanist educators fill the schools with the goal of indoctrinating our kids. Liberal media dominates the news waves. Misinformation is everywhere.

The church ought to be a safe haven of truth.

If we focus all of our time, energy, and resources on creating an excellent children's ministry but fail to recognize the true priority of the gospel, we are failing. Remember:

> Save a man and you save a unit; save a boy and you save a multiplication table.[143]

Addition is great, but when it comes to children and the impact their lives can have on our world, multiplication is better.

Let's be ready and prepared when the right time comes, to share the right message.

> *But sanctify the Lord God in your hearts,* ***and always be ready*** *to give a defense to everyone who asks you a reason for the hope that is in you, with meekness and fear . . .* (1 Pet. 3:15; emphasis mine)

The gospel is the answer to the issues in our world.

It is the only answer which can truly save our children.

Don't be distracted by peripheral things.

Keep a gospel emphasis—the only unmoving target in an ever-changing world.

20

The Gospel Content: An Unmoving Target

Hitting a moving target requires practice and skill, so you would think that aiming for a target that never moves would be easier. It would be easier if the target was clear and the way unhindered. There are many things that distract us from our goal, and there is a very active enemy whose entire purpose is to prevent us from reaching that target.

When defining the goal, I think that we would all agree that the primary reason for children's ministry is to see the kids trust in Christ and continue to grow in their relationship with Him. While we might disagree on the way that happens, or the evidence of it happening, that is our desire and ultimate goal.

Everything else is peripheral, a "means to that end."

Most of us would readily agree that other issues can crowd our number one priority to the extent that we no longer make time or have the energy to achieve it. However, I can't think of a more important consideration than to be communicating the gospel clearly and effectively. Spurgeon wrote an entire sermon on children, and he made some excellent points, such as the following quote:

> But when you teach in Sabbath-schools, you are, if it be possible, in a more responsible situation than even the minister occupies. He preaches to grown-up people, to men of judgment, who, if they do not like what he preaches can go somewhere else; but you teach children who have no option of going elsewhere. If you teach the child wrongly, he believes you; if you teach him heresies, he will receive them; what you teach him now, he will never forget.[144]

Is it possible that we are faltering in our priority and responsibility to communicate the gospel with absolute clarity?

Keep It Simple

When teaching children about the gospel, we need to keep it simple, use familiar words, and avoid confusing "religious" and "churchy" vocabulary.

> Using developmentally appropriate language is critical, because otherwise the words will just skip off the top of their head like a rock on water, or worse, be completely misunderstood.

There's a Christian vocabulary we often lapse into, which probably sounds more like a foreign language to most kids. As adults, we have the tendency to overcomplicate things, and too often we make the good news confusing to kids. We aren't sure what to say, so we say it over in different ways, using different terms, and making it sound complex and involved.

The gospel is not complicated. Keep it simple.

Keep It Free

Another temptation is to add additional steps so that we can count the responses and feel that we have made a difference. Some feel pressure from their church or organization to share the numbers of conversions, so we have kids fill out a card, raise their hands, or "walk forward."

The problem is that connecting belief with other actions only serves to confuse children.

Again, these appeals are no doubt well intentioned. However, the key in calling forth a faith response is not to appeal to the will, but to the understanding. The battle is for the mind, not the will.

> *The god of this age has blinded the* ***minds*** *of unbelievers, so that they cannot see the light of the gospel that displays the glory of Christ* . . . (2 Cor. 4:4 NIV; emphasis mine)

We are not trying to get children to do something. We are trying to help them understand the gospel and believe it.

> One particular need that surfaced for some of the children was a proper understanding of the gospel. The children's responses . . . revealed the need for further instruction regarding salvation and the importance of trusting in Christ alone for salvation . . . children must be carefully taught not to tie actions to faith as being what saves a person. . . . Teachers and parents alike must make this point clear . . . [145]

Instead, you could say something like,

"If you are not sure about going to heaven and you would like to talk more about it, come and find me after the lesson."

"If you believed in Jesus for the first time today, that is great news! Please don't keep it a secret, tell someone!"

We need to keep the gospel free!

Nothing added—just the grace of God.

Keep It Clear

I recently completed a survey of nearly 200 children in five different Bible-believing evangelical churches, asking the question, "How do you get to heaven?"

Each child was between the ages of 6-11 years old, and had varying levels of exposure to the church's teaching. Many of them had grown up in the church; however, when asked how to get to heaven . . .

> . . . only 30 of the 200 children were able to explain that it was because Jesus' death on the cross had paid the price for their sins.

Only 30 kids, out of 200!

Other responses included:

"Because I believe in Jesus" (which is close, but is lacking in content).

"Because I'm a good person."

"I don't know."

These were children who regularly attended church. That should give us pause.

How effective is our teaching if so many children don't know the meaning of the free gift of salvation?

What would the kids in your children's ministry say if you asked them the same question? I tried to garner answers from other churches in the experiment but several of them weren't willing to ask the question. Why wouldn't we want to ask the question unless we are afraid of the answer?

The most important thing is to communicate the gospel in a way that kids understand. Our goal is a simple acceptance of God's gift of eternal life because of what Jesus did for them on the cross.

Young children generally believe what they are told without questioning whether it is true, so we must take care what we teach!

Give it a try and ask the question of the children in your kid's ministry.

Keep It Concrete

Recently, I heard someone say to a first-grader,

"I was walking far away from God . . . and he caught my attention and pulled me back."

We must remember that kids at this age still think concretely and might actually be picturing a man on a dog leash and God yanking him back. We need to explain concepts in a way that ties in to their concrete experience and avoid analogies and symbolic language.

Avoid the abstract and ambiguous and remain as literal as possible.

Keep It Biblical

One of the "go-to" phrases people use when sharing the gospel is this: "Ask Jesus into your heart. He is knocking on the door. Let Him in."

I've heard it many times. But if you do a bit of checking, the concept of "asking Jesus in" is actually a reference for believers. The closest thing to it in the Bible is found in the book of Revelation.

> *Behold, I stand at the door and knock. If anyone hears My voice and opens the door, I will come in to him and dine with him, and he with Me.* (Rev. 3:20)

The phrase is taken from a letter that was written to the church in Laodicea. The believers were guilty of compromising their faith and were described as "lukewarm." The passage is describing Jesus, wanting to be invited back into fellowship with the believers, not a reference to salvation.

Can God still save people when they ask Him to come into their heart? Of course, He can. But how much better if we explain the good news clearly from the beginning.

The truth is, if you aren't a believer, Jesus doesn't want
to come into your heart.
He wants to give you a new heart!

Some teachers will say,

"Do you want to ask Jesus to be your Lord and Savior?"

What does that mean to a child?

"Have you repented from all of your sins?"

Repentance is something we spend our entire Christian life trying to do. God isn't interested in any promises on our part to reform our lives. He wants to give us a new life when we simply believe His promise!

> Children's ministry is full of formulas for the plan of salvation. Each of them is well intentioned. However, the

> Bible doesn't give us a formula. The Bible doesn't say there are four steps, or ABCs or any other recipe. Formulas might be helpful to the presenter, but they can be dangerous to a child . . . Some say, "Come to Christ." What does that mean to a child? Others say, "Give your heart to Jesus." Where is faith in that idea? . . . as presenters we have a responsibility to be as clear and biblically accurate as possible. We will confuse and mislead far fewer children if we are.[146]

Some think that debating the small details in a gospel presentation is unnecessary or even detrimental. We hear the phrase "God is able to use our mistakes." That is definitely true; however, stories are plentiful of people who have wasted years of their lives believing the wrong message or some who even walked away altogether.

> Even though God has undoubtedly saved people despite the countless unclear or flawed gospel presentations over the years, that should not be an excuse for not striving to be biblically clear.

One teacher was recently overheard using Romans 10:9 (a very commonly used verse) to tell his class that even though they "believed" in Jesus for salvation, they also needed to publicly confess Him.

On another occasion, a lady my husband knew heard about several children who had believed in Jesus for salvation. She was extremely concerned and wanted to know, "But have they confessed with their mouth?"

At age 19, prior to his conversion, my husband was told by a well-meaning Christian friend that he was "on the road to hell." When asked why, the friend replied, "I saw you getting off your motorcycle and going into the bar." After assessing this explanation, he concluded it wasn't worth exchanging one "religion" with a set of rules (he was Roman Catholic) for another one (his friend was Baptist).

He continued in his "sinful" lifestyle and unbelief for another seven years before hearing a clear presentation of the gospel. At age 26, he trusted Christ and went on to full-time pastoral ministry.

What might have been accomplished of eternal consequence in those lost seven years? We will never know.

> I give you a solemn admonition on every child's behalf. Surely, if it be murder to administer poison to the dying, it must be far more criminal to give poison to the young life. If it be evil to mislead grey-headed age, it must be far more so to turn aside the feet of the young into the road of error, in which they may forever walk.[147]

Our enemy's goal is to steal, kill, and destroy. We don't need to add fuel to the fire by confusing the message and unwittingly assisting him as he "blinds the minds" of those we are trying to reach.

Let's strive to keep it simple! Keep it free! Keep it clear! Keep it concrete and keep it biblical!

21

Address the Issues: Tackling the Tough Questions

Are you familiar with the issues that our children are facing today?

Closing your eyes to the world's problems might be the easiest route, but God wants us to fight.

Be strong and put on His armor. Wrap yourself in His Truth. Clothe yourself in His righteousness. Surround yourself with His peace. Shield your mind with His salvation. Carry His sword for protection (Eph. 6:10-18).

Nowhere does it say to "run"! Face forward and fight. Teach your students to fight! Be ready to give them biblical answers to their questions.

If given the opportunity, children will ask plenty of hard questions. We need to be prepared with appropriate answers so that we are not caught off guard or overreact. Sometimes, we view questions as an interruption to our lesson plan, when in fact we should invite questions. We should commend the child for having the courage to ask a question and let them know that we are proud of them for thinking well.

We need to provide answers or they will go looking for the answers elsewhere.

One of the primary reasons for young people leaving the church is because they feel that the church has become irrelevant. They think that the church is "ignoring the problems of the real world." If children and young people do not feel that the church can answer their questions, why are we here?

"Faith is not relevant to my career or interests."

"Churches are out of step with the scientific world we live in."

"Christianity is anti-science."

Where are they getting these ideas?[148]

Kids have questions—a lot of questions.

Twenty-nine percent of kids today say they have a hard time believing that a good God would allow so much evil and suffering in the world.[149] Do we have an answer for them?

Forty-six percent of Gen Z kids say they need factual evidence to support their beliefs.[150] Are we providing evidence which satisfies their curiosity and doubts?

If we don't provide that guidance and a foundation for their beliefs, who will? They will find answers. But where are they looking?

Our kids and today's young adults should be looking for answers from the church. However, Gen Z and Gen Alpha kids instead want to know why they should trust a God whose world is ravaged by war, violence, injustice, natural disasters, pain, and suffering. Meanwhile, we are giving them cute, Christian stereotypical responses that aren't enough.

It's time for the church to step up and raise up a generation who knows and believes that absolute truth is found in a proven, trustworthy book—the Bible. We need to train a generation to defend what they believe and be able to lead others to that same faith.

Absolute Truth

The question of absolute truth must be addressed first; otherwise, everything that follows will be in question.

Our children are growing up in a culture which tells them that what is true for you is different than what is true for me. There is no right and wrong, and there are no absolute standards.

If it feels good, do it.

Truth is however you define it.

Faith is fine, if it works for you.

We judge an ethical action based on the situation, not an unchanging universal code of conduct. Everything is grey and dependent upon the lens we are looking through. To think otherwise is to be actively working against love, tolerance, and equality. This is not to say that everything in life and the Bible is black and white, but I think we can all agree that grey is not typically the rule.

How do we address this idea of relative truth?

While the world tells us that everything is relative, that is not exactly accurate. Everyone believes in some level of absolute truth, even if they don't want to admit it.

We all agree that murder is wrong. To believe this, we must have accepted some level of truth, some definition of good and evil.

If you pose a question regarding the crime of torturing or bullying a child, you'll find it difficult to find anyone (even someone who promotes relativism) who believes that it is acceptable to do that. Ask a husband who is a proponent of no absolute truth if he's okay with his wife having an affair. Ask those who support abolishing the death penalty what they would do if their family member was brutally murdered. If someone admits that they "enjoy" killing people, I doubt that you would find support for that even in our relativistic world.

> Everyone has a limit to their "relativism".
> If you press them, they will eventually have to admit that all beliefs have consequences. There will be fallout eventually, and "truth" will be there in the end. Back them into a corner, and that's where we find truth.
> That's where we find God.

We need to demonstrate this with our children.

The Tough Questions

Once you've re-established truth, then we can talk about the other issues. Most parents and guardians want the church to help them deal with the tough topics:

Current events, mental health, depression, anxiety, bullying, loneliness, social media, caring for the environment, racial inequality, suicide, self-harm, school shootings, politics, sexuality, gender identity and inequality, abortion, and so many others.

Do we have answers for these issues?

With all that technology offers in the way of visual stimuli, growing up in a culture that emphasizes sex over love leaves our youth struggling with how they are to respond, especially as marriage is more commonly delayed. How do I maintain my sexual purity in this culture?

> Research indicates that most young Christians are as sexually active as their non-Christian peers, even though they are more conservative in their attitudes about sexuality. One-sixth of young Christians (17%) said they "have made mistakes and feel judged in church because of them." The issue of sexuality is particularly salient among 18 to 29-year-old Catholics, among whom two out of five (40%) said the church's "teachings on sexuality and birth control are out of date.[151]

Where should they go for answers?

I don't recall the last sermon given on purity and sex before marriage, do you?

Where can they go when they have honest questions?

If your young adults come to you to admit a mistake, don't let your response be the reason they never set foot in a church again. While we are called upon to preach truth and promote the lifestyle Jesus designed, we are not called to judge or shame. Be compassion personified!

> Young adults with Christian experience say the church is not a place that allows them to express doubts. They do not feel safe admitting that sometimes Christianity does not make sense . . . Some of the perceptions in this regard include not being able "to ask my most pressing life questions in church" (36%) and having "significant intellectual doubts about my faith" (23%).[152]

What do we say when they have spiritual questions?

- How do you know God is real?
- How do you know Jesus rose from the dead?
- Why are there over 4,000 religions?

- Are you sure creation really happened, or does evolution make more sense?
- How do we know the Bible is God's Word?
- Why does God allow disease, crime, and natural disasters to bring so much suffering, damage, and even death?
- What about people who never get to hear about Jesus?

Then there are the personal questions.

- Who am I?
- How should I live in this world?
- Do my choices really matter?
- Does my life matter?
- Am I loved?
- Does anyone care?
- Can I make a difference?

If you can't answer these questions, you need to think about it and be prepared.

There might come times when some of the issues raised are beyond our level of expertise. For example, if we discover that a child is engaging in self-harm, or if reference is made concerning a friend who is considering suicide, we need to exercise caution and discernment, recognizing when we are out of our depth and when to refer families to a professional.

We should never attempt to assume the role of a psychologist or therapist. In those scenarios, always consult an expert, especially if you believe the child is a danger to themselves or others.

Invincible and Indestructible

"I have plenty of time. For now, I'm going to enjoy my life, and I'll think about God when I'm older." Have you ever heard this kind of thinking?

A good friend tells a story of his life as a young unbeliever. He lived as he wanted, with little thought for the consequences of his actions and no interest in spiritual matters. That is, until his best friend died. His death really shook him up and resulted in his search—and discovery—of God.

Death doesn't discriminate. Coffins come in all sizes. Kids today might think that they are invincible and indestructible, but they aren't.

We need to be ready to talk about issues like this.

> Unfortunately, curriculums do not usually cover these issues, and most children's ministry leaders and teachers often don't feel comfortable level engaging with these difficult social issues.

They wonder,

"Is this something parents and guardians will be okay with me discussing with their children?" "What is the right age and right context to tackle this with a student?"

"Am I knowledgeable or confident enough to lead this discussion or answer questions?"

"Is this something to be handled as a whole class, in small groups or individually?"

Touchy subjects should be open for discussion in church programs for kids; but unfortunately, the leaders don't always feel ready or equipped.

If we want to be relevant, we must engage in the issues our children are being confronted with daily. Initiate discussions that cause kids to grapple with the questions and find the answers together.

If they can work through these questions while they are young, it will give them a solid foundation where they can build their faith.

We must prepare kids by helping them find the answers to the hard questions they will face as they grow up. If we do not, their faith will wilt away under the pressure of a culture that does not believe in absolute truth.

Consult the Experts

The church could provide links to helpful podcasts, make time for training opportunities for parents, provide support and counseling resources for those struggling with mental health issues, and allow for regular feedback where church leaders can find out what parents need.

Why not create short, sharable videos answering questions like who is Jesus, why the Bible matters, or how to let go of anger? What if you talked about money, vocation, life's purpose, burnout, or anxiety? Create tools and content you can share throughout the week that have the chance to reach people at home or at work. Research the materials that are available on apologetics and hard questions; they do exist and can be helpful.

We need to remember that these gaps in teaching don't necessarily need to be filled with the input of children's ministers and volunteers alone—additional training can be helpful; special guests invited to speak on certain topics and resources abound on the internet in the form of websites, blogs, and books.[153] We cannot be expected to be experts on every topic.

Sound Theologians

The very least we must do is to be ready to apply a biblical lens over whatever message comes to our kids from the culture.

Children should not be taught something that must later be adjusted, and we need to be clear on our Bible skills and interpretations. We must train kids to assess the counterfeit by recognizing the truth.

If you don't feel equipped, perhaps it means enrolling in a course at a Bible school or seminary, but whatever it takes, we must increase our knowledge base to avoid common mistakes like pulling verses out of context or misapplying them.

> Kids leaders might not be thought of as theologians by many people, but I believe we should be some of the most sound theologians in the church. We play such an important role in establishing theological foundations in our kids, and those foundations have to be made out of rock, not sand. If our theology is weak as leaders, we are virtually dooming our kids to have a shaky theology as well.[154]

Many of us in leadership have little to no Bible training. Perhaps we were elementary teachers in a former life, or just a committed, enthusiastic volunteer. But having a base level of theological training is critical.

> Most of the children's ministry leaders I know haven't had much in the way of formal ministry training. Few have studied children's ministry in college or seminary. Most haven't gone to a single children's ministry workshop.[155]

Spurgeon stated it very well: "Have a care what you are after; you are teaching children, mind what you teach them. Put poison in the spring, and it will pollute the whole stream . . . Have a care, it is a child's soul you are tampering with . . . it is a child's soul you are preparing for eternity . . . "[156]

Keep learning.

Keep growing.

Search for the answers to the tough questions which are bombarding our children head on.

Be ready to give a defense.

Offer the only alternative that will lead to truth and hope.

Be the confident voice of reason and shelter from this dark world.

Address the issues.

22

The Millstone Warning: Do Not Hinder Them

During my time in kid's ministry, I learned two things (that I already knew): children are precious in God's sight and this was the time to reach them for Christ. Bible narratives include stories of dozens of children and make it clear that God loves children and that they are a gift from God.[157]

We know the biblical commands and the statistics, and it's what drives us as we assume this responsibility of children's ministry leadership with all of its stresses and complications. We know that the most receptive years are 4-14, and that reaching a child during these years can potentially save them, not only from an eternity without God but also from a lifetime of poor decisions and devastating consequences.

The Bible, on the other hand, speaks about some devastating consequences for those who don't value these precious ones.

Most of us have no doubt read the verses,

"Do not offend them."
"Do not despise them."
"Do not forbid them."

Sandwiched in between these commands is the story of the lost sheep and the example of the shepherd who searches until he finds it!

Scripture talks about the consequences of leading a child astray or doing things which would prevent children from coming to Christ.

That is something we would rather not think about. In fact, in all of my reading and research over the years, I have never read anything about how that happens.

What does that mean?

What is done, or not done, that qualifies as offending, hindering, or forbidding?

I think it's clear that one way would be to disregard and neglect the needs of children, and those of us who have dedicated our lives to serving children would obviously not fall into that category. But are there other ways that we could be guilty?

Do Not Offend One

In the book of Matthew, Jesus had just finished a series of miracles[158] and the disciples no doubt expected that He was tired. They decided, without consulting the Master, that they would try to protect Him from further intrusions, but they clearly did not understand His mission.[159] The disciples were discussing, (or perhaps arguing might be more appropriate) who was the greatest in the kingdom of heaven. Jesus stated that one who is humble is the greatest, and He used the example of a child to illustrate His point.

He called a little child over, placed him right in the middle of the discussion, and then gave a very serious admonition:

> *"If anyone causes one of these little ones—those who believe in me—to stumble, it would be better for them to have a large millstone hung around their neck and to be drowned in the depths of the sea."* (Matt. 18:6 NIV)[160]

The word described here is more accurately the "upper millstone" which might be as much as 1.5 m (5 ft) in diameter and would be turned on the top of an even larger, lower stationary stone. A domestic animal, such as a donkey, would turn the upper stone to grind grain or crush olives. It was very different from the typical small hand mill used by women for grinding grain.[161]

It was an extreme statement made to emphasize the point.

Those listening would have understood and would realize

that the consequence referred to is death. Hanging a millstone around one's neck and being thrown into the sea was a form of capital punishment in Egypt, Rome, and Greece during the time of Christ, and punishment by drowning in this manner was no doubt a familiar reference.[162]

Causing a child to stumble was considered serious enough to warrant being drowned as a consequence. What does it mean to "offend" or to "cause to stumble"?

The verb used by Matthew is "*skandalizo,*" which he used on thirteen different occasions. It can mean, "to offend, to cause to fall or to ensnare in a trap."[163] It is used here in Matthew 18:6 in an "active" sense, meaning to "cause someone" to fall away from (or reject) faith. How does this happen? How could someone cause a person, or in this case, a child, to stumble?

Do Not Despise One

Jesus continues, again warning His disciples, "Do not despise 'one.'" Do not despise a child.

> *"Take heed that you* ***do not despise one*** *of these little ones, for I say to you that in heaven their angels always see the face of My Father who is in heaven."* (Matt. 18:10; emphasis mine)

"Despise" is also used in Matthew 6:24 and can be translated as "to look down on" or "Make sure you never consider one of these little ones as unimportant."[164]

Jesus loved investing in the less fortunate or social outcasts. There are many times in Scripture—for example, the disfigured leper, the unpopular tax collector, the demon possessed man, the blind beggar, and even an unsavory prostitute—where Jesus cares for those who were usually shunned or disregarded by those around them.[165]

Scripture makes it clear that we are to remember the example of Jesus and not look down on any child! Don't play favorites. Love them all.

Do Not Lose One

He immediately follows these exhortations with a parable, which portrays a man who owns one hundred sheep and while he's in the field, one wanders away. He immediately leaves the ninety-nine to look for the one which is missing.

> *If a man has a hundred sheep, and one of them goes astray, does he not leave the ninety-nine and go to the mountains to seek the one that is straying?* (Matt. 18:12)

Like the good shepherd, God values each one of us and will do whatever it takes to seek us out and save us.

Notice that the shepherd doesn't boast about his ability to retain ninety-nine or the fact that he has ninety-nine.

He doesn't blame the sheep for not following and getting lost, and he doesn't blame someone else for losing it.

Instead, he drops what he's doing and takes the time to find it. His focus is entirely on the one!

How many times have we seen a child stop attending?

Do we stop to ask why?

Do we stop to ask ourselves if our behavior or teaching contributed to their leaving?

Harsh words perhaps with a child who repeatedly misbehaves?

Showing more attention and favor to the attractive, sweet mannered children at the expense of the poorly dressed, sullen boy?

It is our solemn responsibility to love each one of those who have been entrusted to us. The welfare of every child, small or great, is a matter of vital importance.

A shepherd's heart is one who pursues the child who has strayed.

How did he know that one of his sheep was missing?

He counted them.

He knew them.

How often do we scan our attendance system for missing children? Do we keep accurate records and have a system that notifies us of absences? Are we making sure that our check-in teams are collecting accurate contact information when new families register? Do we have a follow-up procedure in place for absent kids? In our busyness, do we stop and look for them when they are missing?

Do Not Forbid/Hinder One

In the next chapter, the disciples are given a second warning. Apparently, they had already forgotten what Jesus said earlier about the worth of a child and the seriousness of causing them to stumble.

> *Then little children were brought to Him that He might put His hands on them and pray, but the disciples rebuked them.* (Matt. 19:13)

Some parents arrived while the disciples were questioning Jesus on the issue of divorce. They brought their little children with them, no doubt hoping that Jesus would lay His hands upon their children in blessing, as was a recognized Jewish tradition.[166] The disciples' response was an indictment on their attitudes. Roy Zuck says in his book *Precious in His Sight*:

> Thinking young children would be a nuisance to the Lord, the disciples rebuked ("to reprove, censure, or threaten")

those who brought their youngsters. The disciples wanted to stop them from disturbing Jesus, possibly because they thought he was too busy, too tired, or unconcerned. The disciples reproved the parents because they believed their actions were improper, and because Jewish adults considered it a waste to spend time with children.[167]

Jesus made it very clear that he was not happy with their behavior.

But when Jesus saw it, He was ***greatly displeased*** *. . .* (Mark 10:14; emphasis mine)

I love Spurgeon's quote:

He [Jesus] was not often displeased; certainly, He was not often "much displeased," and when He was much displeased, we may be sure that the case was serious. He was displeased at these children being pushed away from Him, for it was so contrary to His mind about them. The disciples did wrong to the mothers; they rebuked the parents for doing a motherly act—for doing, in fact, that which Jesus loved them to do. They brought their children to Jesus out of respect to Him . . . He was therefore much displeased to think that those good women, who meant Him honor, should be roughly repulsed.[168]

He rebuked the disciples again, and then revealed his love and affection for those children by taking them in his arms, placing his hands on them, and blessing them.

But Jesus said, "Let the little children come to Me, and ***do not forbid*** *them; for of such is the kingdom of heaven." And He laid His hands on them . . . "* (Matt. 19:13-15; emphasis mine)[169]

The words "forbid" or "hinder" are used interchangeably amongst different translations. The Greek word is "*kōlyō*" ("κωλύω") meaning "to hinder, to prevent, to impede, or forbid" and it appears 23 times in the New Testament.

What could be defined as hindering?

How might we be impeding a child from coming to Jesus?

- Could it be that having our priorities messed up might be a hindrance?
- Focusing on the "wow" more than relationships?
- Valuing the wrong things?
- Teaching without being properly prepared?
- Confusing the gospel or complicating the message of salvation?
- Setting a bad example by proudly striving for selfish interests?
- Failing to partner well with parents?
- Were there children who visited, felt unwelcome, out of place or bored, and never returned?

Could these actions be reason for concern?

Is there something we are doing that might be offending one? Despising one? Losing one? Hindering one?

Is it possible that we might be guilty of this? Surely not.

We have devoted our lives to children's ministry and spend every waking moment strategizing and planning for them.

This is serious stuff. May it never be that we contributed to a child "stumbling" over their belief or inhibiting their ability to reach the Savior because something trips him up.

23

Recognize the Signs: The Reality of "Burnout"

I can testify that children's ministry leadership is no picnic.

"Overtime" is "all the time."

From January to December, the calendar never stops.

From morning to night, there is always something needed.

Can you relate?

I believe that children's ministry is the most demanding ministry in the church. Have you ever noticed?

- Children's ministry is typically serving the largest groups of people in the church: children, parents, and volunteers. Each requires encouragement and attention.
- You are serving the most vulnerable, who are at the highest risk for physical harm, emotional injury, and opportunity for criminal activity.
- Children are the most spiritually impressionable, yet the least able to manage themselves.

- Newborn through preteen entails the greatest physical, social, emotional, and mental/developmental span, necessitating the most specific and wide-ranging volunteer training and the most diverse range of teaching materials.
- Children's ministry demands the most unique and varied ministry environments with the greatest amount of weekly maintenance (sanitizing toys, organizing teaching supplies and managing multiple environments).
- You are working with the single most precious part of a family's life—their children.
- And lastly, despite the demand, children's ministry is typically one of the most underfunded departments in the church in terms of salary and resources.

Working with children may be the least understood or appreciated ministry in the church. Most churchgoers and even other staff have no idea of the demands of this constantly changing ministry.

All of this running can be grueling. Some of us are determined to keep running, no matter how dehydrated and exhausted we have become. "Never give up" is our mantra.

That's a great recipe for burnout and the end of our kid's ministry career. If you think you can run on empty, you are sorely misinformed. No one can!

The Reality of "Burnout"

If you have lost your focus, if you have you lost your joy, if you find yourself constantly speaking negatively about your church, you may be experiencing burnout.

"Burnout" has been defined as a combination of emotional exhaustion, a depleted ability to care and a decreased sense of accomplishment.[170] Barna sees indications of burnout risk among children's ministry leaders:

> Collectively, children's ministry leaders show signs of all three in Barna's research. They describe feeling unsure of their long-term impact, fearing that kids will walk away from the faith and not knowing how to gauge their effectiveness. Their work-life balance is at risk. "They often feel siloed from the rest of the church and ministry or like they don't have what they need to do a job they see as very important.[171]

That's scary! I've seen burnout up close and it's becoming more common.

Healthy boundaries must be in place for your survival!

- Protect your daily time with the Lord—make it a priority.
- Ensure a regular dose of encouragement—listen to a podcast on the way to church.
- Prioritize your friendships. Schedule times for coffee or lunch.
- Attend worship or catch a sermon as often as you can.
- Take your day off seriously. Don't answer emails, phone calls, or texts!
- Get some rest. Don't hesitate to take a nap, especially after those grueling seasonal special events.
- Plan short retreats where you can leave town for a day or two and refresh your perspective.

- Try to continue with at least one fun hobby that you had prior to beginning your job.
- Determine that you will work only as much as God asks and no more.
- Take a real vacation with your family and leave your phone on silent.

The calendar is always rotating around those seasonal events, but they should be exceptions to the normal pace of work and be balanced by compensating rest.

Allow the Lord to carry you through those times when you feel like you have nothing left to give. If your load feels impossible to carry, it is likely you are attempting more than He is asking of you.

It is Not Your Ministry

The fastest way to drown in stress is to forget that the ministry belongs to God.

Remember: It's not your ministry

God started it and will sustain it.

He can run it without you.

The best solution for the stresses you experience is to give the ministry back to God and remember it was always His to begin with.

Work hard with the calm assurance that you can only do what you can do, and the rest is up to God.

You can't spill what you don't carry.

Success depends on Him.

> *Come to Me, all you who labor and are heavy laden, and I will give you rest. Take My yoke upon you and learn from Me, for I am gentle and lowly in heart, and you will find rest for*

your souls. For My yoke is easy and My burden is light." (Matt. 11:28-30)

You are Not Alone

It's very easy to feel alone, unsupported, and isolated in ministry. Stepping into a full-time staff position often leaves you feeling disconnected and alone.

Your pastor is now your boss.

Your elders are your accountability.

Your friends are your volunteers.

You are on our own, sink or swim.

It's critical for us to maintain at least one or two good friendships outside of our ministry. Someone you can trust, someone that you can vent to knowing that it won't be repeated.

Seek out a mentor from a neighboring church, someone who can encourage you and help you regain your focus when you need it.

As iron sharpens iron, so a man sharpens the countenance of his friend. (Prov. 27:17)

Do you have a friend? You may not survive without one!

If you feel out of control, you may need to consult further help.

If you have a "take it or leave it" attitude about your ministry, if your family or friends are worried, or if you become more angry or emotional than usual, it may be time for a break.

If you have withdrawn from things that bring you joy because you just don't have time anymore, get help!

Don't ignore the signs of an empty tank.

If this feels all too familiar, seek help from a trusted counselor. Healing is possible!

Find a friend or counselor (outside of your church) that you can talk to without the fear of being judged. Let them help you define some boundaries and hold you accountable.

Recovery is possible!

> *And He said to me, "My grace is sufficient for you, for My strength is made perfect in weakness."* (2 Cor. 12:9)

24

Staying the Course: Never Surrender

Children's ministry isn't for wimps; it is hard work. There are challenges. Remember that nothing worthwhile comes easily! We need to stay the course!

Remember Your Calling

Remember when you first began in children's ministry?

Remember when you knew that the Lord was leading you to work with children?

Remember when it was about reaching lost kids and discipling those who had trusted Christ?

You knew that God was telling you to work with children.

You knew that you were in the right place.

It all sounded so clear! How about now?

It's easy to forget Timothy's message in the midst of all of the other messages.

> *Therefore, I remind you to stir up the gift of God which is in you through the laying on of my hands.* (2 Tim. 1:6)

If you want to go the distance, you will need the certainty of God's call.

The first "honeymoon" year will end.

Criticism and hurt will be inevitable, and the stress will beat you down.

There will always be pressure knowing that families will leave and go elsewhere.

The initial excitement for the ministry will tarnish.

No amount of training prepares us for the demands of the ministry. But being sure of your calling and walking alongside the promises of the Lord's presence and strength can sustain you.

> *But none of these things move me; nor do I count my life dear to myself, so that I may finish my race with joy, and the ministry* ***which I received from the Lord Jesus****, to testify to the gospel of the grace of God.* (Acts 20:24; emphasis mine)

Have you forgotten how clear it sounded?

How sure you were that you were in the right place?

Is the clarity gone?

Remember your calling!

Remember the Vision

Do you remember the why?

Do you remember the reason for your commitment to children's ministry?

We're raising up a generation of disciples. We're changing the world, one child at a time.

That 4-14 window is still open. The children you are working with are ripe for the harvest. When the going gets tough, it helps to remember the reason for the work you are doing.

Where there is no vision, the people perish. (Prov. 29:18 KJV)

One of the greatest tools the enemy uses is discouragement.

- Do you ever get tired of dealing with kids who don't seem to listen, or volunteers who don't show up?
- Parents who treat you like a free babysitter, or the take home papers you lovingly created that end up on the ground outside or in a trashcan?
- Feeling like you're at the end of your rope? Wondering if anything you are doing is making a difference?
- Want to quit every Monday morning?

Losing sight of the finish line will inevitably lead to discouragement.

Remember the window!

That small time of greatest opportunity.

Keep your eye on the goal.

Therefore, my beloved brethren, be steadfast, immovable, always abounding in the work of the Lord, knowing that your labor is not in vain in the Lord. (1 Cor. 15:58)

You are never wasting your time when you serve the Lord.

When the "thank you" comments are few and far between, and when the discouragements threaten to overtake you, remember the vision.

Remember Your Audience

A former supervisor told me once that he was pleased with the job I was doing because it "made him look good". That wasn't the reason I was working as hard as I was.

> *And whatever you do, do it heartily, as to the Lord and not to men, knowing that from the Lord you will receive the reward of the inheritance; for you serve the Lord Christ.* (Col. 3:23-24)

I'm sure that you often feel as though you've had enough, but remember your Audience.

It is not the parents or your pastor.

You are working for the Lord.

He knows your heart and your motives.

Remember the end goal: the eternal inheritance waiting for you.

> *I do all this for the sake of the gospel, that I may share in its blessings. Do you not know that in a race all the runners run, but only one gets the prize? Run in such a way as to get the prize.*" (1 Cor. 9:23-24 NIV)

Run your race well. Be diligent when no one is watching.

Our service is for an audience of One, the Lord Jesus Christ.

While your boss may think he's in charge, he is not your final authority.

You are not working for him.

You are working for the One who loves kids.

The King of the Universe.

> *And let us not grow weary while doing good, for in due season, we shall reap if we do not lose heart.* (Gal. 6:9)

Remember the Enemy

Focus on reminding yourself to fight the right enemy.

It's not the leadership!

For many of us, we lead the children's ministry on a staff of mostly men, at least that was my situation. I did not enjoy the comradery they felt and was usually not invited to the quick lunches or coffee breaks. I usually felt outnumbered and alone.

It's not the congregation!

It's so easy to focus on ourselves and point the finger at everyone else. We might not be able to control our circumstances, but we can choose how we react, our perspective, and the people we trust.

It's not even church politics.

Yes, it stinks and should not be found inside the walls of a family who love each other. But it's not the real enemy.

Too often we forget what we should hold onto, and we hold onto the things we should forget.

> *So do not fear, for I am with you; do not be dismayed, for I am your God. I will strengthen you and help you; I will uphold you with my righteous right hand.* (Isa. 41:10)

Draw your strength from a loving Savior who earnestly desires to meet us at the point of our greatest need.

25
Conclusion

Don't Give Up!

You may not feel capable or qualified for the job. That's okay.

God is in the business of using people whose greatest qualification is simply His calling, His strength and the willingness to answer and follow.

Look at the disciples: they were young, inexperienced, and at times, they acted immaturely! But they were teachable and through them, God changed the world!

God has called you.

He will lead you.

He will provide.

He will build you as you seek to build the ministry to reach and teach kids for Him!

Someone recently shared this letter of commissioning, which she keeps in a frame on the wall of her office at church, and I thought it was a great reminder:

> I acknowledge and accept the commission given to me by my Lord and Savior Jesus Christ. Understanding

> that the enemy is deceptive and determined, I remain confident, courageous, and committed to the mission and accept my specific role and responsibilities. I will allow no enemy, seen or unseen, to distract, diminish, or destroy the destiny that awaits me. Though I may feel fear, I will not be controlled by fear. But with faith, I will move forward, trusting my God, and will embrace the overwhelming victory that has been promised by the One who commissioned me.
>
> *But those who wait on the Lord shall renew their strength; They shall mount up with wings like eagles. They shall run and not be weary. They shall walk and not faint.* (Isa. 40:31)

We serve a risen Savior. He is the King of Kings and Lord of Lords. He is sovereign over all. The adversary might be devious and powerful, but we know how the story ends. Don't give up. Don't lose heart. Remember God's heart for kids.

Unless we adjust in our children's ministry, we can potentially lose an entire generation. We can't allow that to happen. This generation needs us! They might be unique, but they are also still kids, and they need Jesus.

> Want to enter God's Kingdom? Then become like little children.
>
> Want to be great in God's eyes? Then become like little children.
>
> Want to let Jesus know you welcome and receive him? Then welcome little children.
>
> Want to avoid judgment at God's hands? Then don't lead little children astray.

Want to identify with God's plans? Then don't belittle or despise little children.

Want to avoid rebuke from Jesus? Then don't prevent children from coming to him.

Want to follow Jesus' example of love? Then love, pray for, accept, be with, and bless little children.[172]

We have the best job ever. What a privilege it is to work with kids.

And he said, "Truly I tell you, unless you change and become like little children, you will never enter the kingdom of heaven. Therefore, whoever takes the lowly position of this child is the greatest in the kingdom of heaven. And whoever welcomes one such child in My name welcomes Me." (Matt. 18:3-5 NIV)

We must gain an understanding of our children so that we can call them in from the world in which they are playing.

We must proclaim a message which is relevant to their needs, grabs their attention, and breaks the magnetic attraction of our ever-darkening world.

We must help them to experience God for themselves and do whatever it takes to restore their trust and belief.

Nighttime is approaching, but the fireflies are still glowing.

There is still time to warn them of the dangers lurking in the swamps and forest.

Call them in while they are still listening.

Call them in before it gets too dark.

Call them in before it's too late.

Call them in before they are gone.

When you see fireflies!

THANK YOU FOR READING MY BOOK!

I really appreciate all of your feedback, and
I love hearing what you have to say.
I need your input to make the next version of this book and
my future books better.
Please leave me a helpful review on Amazon letting me
know what you thought of the book.
Thanks so much!!
—Janine McNally

You can email me at janine@grace4kidz.org and connect with us on:

Facebook: https://www.facebook.com/Grace4Kidz
Instagram: https://www.instagram.com/grace4kidz/
Twitter: https://twitter.com/JTMcNally
Pinterest: https://www.pinterest.com/Grace4Kidz/

Bibliography and Recommended Reading

Adams, Steve, *Children's Ministry on Purpose: A Purpose Driven Approach to Lead Kids Toward Spiritual Health*, Grand Rapids, MI: Zondervan, 2017.

Anthony, M. Ed. *Perspectives on Children's Spiritual Formation: Four views.* Nashville, TN: Broadman &Holman. 2006.

Barna, George. *Children's Ministry in a New Reality Building Church Communities That Cultivate Lasting Faith*, 2022

__________. *Guiding Children to Discover the Bible, Navigate Technology & Follow Jesus How Ministry Leaders & Parents Partner in Faith Formation* 2020

__________. *Transforming Children into Spiritual Champions.* Ventura, CA: Regal Books, 2003.

Bastian, Karl, *Kidology's Ultimate Toolbox for Children's Ministry* Peabody, MA. Hendrickson Publishing Group. RoseKidz 2018.

Beckwith, Ivy. *Formational Children's Ministry: Shaping Children Using Story, Ritual, and Relationship.* Grand Rapids, MI: Baker Books. 2010.

Bell, Valerie, *Resilient, Child Discipleship and the Fearless Future of the Church.* Marceline, MO: Walsworth Pub. Co. 2020

Dembowczyk, Brian, *Gospel-Centered Kids Ministry* Nashville, TN: Lifeway Press, 2017.

DeVries, Mark and Annette Safstrom, *Sustainable Children's Ministry—From Last-Minute Scrambling to Long-Term Solutions,* Downers Grove, IL: InterVarsity Press, 2018.

Elmore, Tim; McPeak, Andrew. *Generation Z Unfiltered: Facing Nine Hidden Challenges of the Most Anxious Population* Atlanta, GA: Poet Gardner. 2019 Kindle Edition.

Fowler, Larry. *Rock-Solid Children's Ministry: Biblical Principles that Will Transform Your Ministry* Bloomington, MN: Bethany House Publishers, 2013.

___________. *Rock-Solid Kids: Giving Children a Biblical Foundation for Life* Bloomington, MN: Bethany House Publishers, 2005.

Houser, Tina, *Building Children's Ministry: A Practical Guide.* Nashville, TN: Thomas Nelson Inc. 2008.

Hudson, Dale *Fertile Soil, See Kid's Faith Grow and Flourish for A Lifetime.* Dale Hudson www.buildingchildrensministry.com, 2022.

Jutila, Craig., et al. *Children's Ministry That Works!* Loveland, CO: Group Publishing. 2002.

___________. Jim Wideman, et al. *Children's Ministry in the 21st Century.* Loveland, CO: Group Publishing. 2007.

Lovaglia, Dan. *Relational Children's Ministry. Turning Kid-Influencers into Lifelong Disciple Makers.* Grand Rapids, MI: Zondervan, 2016.

McConnell, Douglas, Jennifer Orona, and Paul Stockley. *Understanding God's Heart for Children: Toward a Biblical Framework.* Independently Published, 2019.

McCrindle, Mark, Fell, Ashley & Buckerfield, Sam, *Generation Alpha. Understanding our Children and Helping them Thrive.* Hachette Australia. Kindle Edition.

McCrindle, M., & Wolfinger, E. (2009). *The ABC of XYZ: Understanding the Global Generations.*

Murrow, David, *Why Men Hate Going to Church.* Nashville, TN: Thomas Nelson, 2002.

Powell, Kara E. and Chap Clark. *Sticky Faith Everyday Ideas to Build Lasting Faith in Your Kids.* Grand Rapids, MI: Zondervan, 2011.

Sweet, Sean, *Let Go and Run Beside: Essentials of Intentional Preteen Ministry.* Four Rivers Design, 2020.

Twenge, J. M. *iGen: Why Today's Super-Connected Kids Are Growing Up Less Rebellious, More Tolerant, Less Happy—And Completely Unprepared for Adulthood—And What That Means for The Rest of Us.* New York: Atria Books, 2017.

Washinton, Valora. *Changing the Game for Generation Alpha, Teaching and Raising Young Children in the 21st Century.* St. Paul, MN: Redleaf Press. 2021

Wideman, Jim. *Children's Ministry Leadership: The You-Can-Do-It Guide.* Loveland, CO: Group Publishing, 2003.

Zuck, Roy B. *Precious in His Sight: Childhood and Children in the Bible.* Grand Rapids, MI: Baker Books, 1996.

Articles and Journals

AAP (2016), American Academy of Pediatrics Announces New Recommendations for Children's Media Use, https://www.aap.org/en-us/about-the-aap/aap-press-room/Pages/American- Academy-of-Pediatrics-Announces-New-Recommendations-for-Childrens-Media-Use.aspx

All4Kids.org Raising Generation Alpha Kids: A Parenting Guide. 10/29/2019 https://www.all4kids.org/news/blog/raising-generation-alpha-kids-a-parenting-guide/

Arora, A. & Jha., A., K. (2020). Understanding pattern of online gaming addiction among Indian teenagers. *Our Heritage, 68*(1), 13190-13100.

Augner, C., & Hacker, G. W. (2012). Associations between problematic mobile phone use and psychological parameters in young adults. *International Journal of Public Health, 57*(2), 437-441.

AWANA Clubs International, "Scriptural Evaluation of Salvation Invitations," 2004. http://www.bible.org/docs/splife/evang/awana.htm

Bologna, Caroline. What's The Deal with Generation Alpha? Updated Sep 25, 2021 https://www.huffpost.com/entry/generation-alpha-after-gen-z_l_5d420ef4e4b0aca341181574

Caplan, S., Williams, D., & Yee, N. (2009). Problematic Internet use and psychosocial well-being among MMO players. *Computers in Human Behavior, 25*(6), 1312-1319.

Carter, C. M. (2016, December 21). *The Complete Guide to Generation Alpha, The Children of Millennials.* Forbes. Retrieved from https://www.forbes.com/sites/christinecarter/2016/12/21/the-complete-guide-to-generation-alpha-the-children-of-millennials/#49b12e303623

Cox, Daniel A. Generation Z and the Future of Faith in America *Survey Center on American Life* March 24, 2022 | https://www.americansurveycenter.org/research/generation-z-future-of-faith/

Dretsch, Heather. *Meet the Mini Millennials: Generation Alpha*, October 1, 2021 https://poole.ncsu.edu/thought-leadership/article/meet-the-mini-millennials-generation-alpha/

Fourtané, Susan. *Generation Alpha: The Children of the Millennial* Dec 18, 2018 https://interestingengineering.com/generation-alpha-the-children-of-the-millennial

Gottschalk, F. (2019). Impacts of technology use on children: Exploring literature on the brain, cognition and well-being. *OECD Education Working Paper No. 195.*

Hinduja, S., & Patchin, J. W. (2014). *Bullying beyond the schoolyard: Preventing and responding to cyberbullying.* Corwin Press.

Ipsos (2018). *Global Views on Cyberbullying.* Retrieved from https://www.ipsos.com/en/global-views-cyberbullying

Jha, A. K., Pandey V., & Kumari, V. (2019). What's eating up Adolescent Sleep? Evidence from Bihar. *Gujarat Research Society, 21*(9).

Keeley, B., & Little, C. (2017). *The State of the World Children 2017: Children in a Digital World.* The United Nations Children's Fund (UNICEF).

Kumar, Amrit Jha, *Understanding Generation Alpha*, June 2020 https://www.researchgate.net/publication/342347030_Understanding_Generation_Alpha?enrichId=rgreq-9da1cd6993764fa1baa9e833824ed461-XXX&enrichSource=Y292ZXJQYWdlOzM0MjM0NzAzMDtBUzo5MjQ2NzA0MDA0MTc3OTJAMTU5NzQ3MDAxMTQ1MQ%3D%3D&el=1_x_2&_esc=publicationCoverPdf

Marty Machowski, God Made Boys and Girls: Helping Children Understand the Gift of Gender, September 2, 2019

Pasquarelli, Adrianne and Schultz, E.J.. *Move Over Gen Z, Generation Alpha Is the One To Watch* January 22, 2019. https://adage.com/article/cmo-strategy/move-gen-z-generation-alpha-watch/316314

Pinsker, Joe. *Oh No, They've Come Up with Another Generation Label How Much Do Members Of "Generation Alpha," Or Any Generation, Really Have in Common?* Feb. 21, 2020 https://www.theatlantic.com/family/archive/2020/02/generation-after-gen-z-named-alpha/606862/

Pitchforth, J., Fahy, K., Ford, T., Wolpert, M., Viner, R. M., & Hargreaves, D. S. (2019). Mental health and well-being trends among children and young people in the UK, 1995–2014: Analysis of repeated cross-sectional national health surveys. *Psychological Medicine, 49*(8), 1275-1285.

Rampell, C. (2015, May 4). *Bad news for older folks: Millennials are having fewer babies.* The Washington Post. Retrieved from https://www.washingtonpost.com/opinions/among-millennials-theres-a-baby-bust/2015/05/04/c98d5a08-f295-11e4-84a6-6d7c67c50db0_story.html

Takeuchi, H., Taki, Y., Hashizume, H., Asano, K., Asano, M., Sassa, Y., Yokota, S., Kotozaki, Y., Nouchi, R. & Kawashima, R. (2016). Impact of videogame play on the brain's microstructural properties: Cross-sectional and longitudinal analyses. *Molecular Psychiatry, 21*(12), 1781-1789.

Tang, S., & Patrick, M. E. (2018). Technology and interactive social media use among 8th and 10th graders in the US and associations with homework and school grades. *Computers in Human Behavior, 86*, 34-44.

Telus International *Generation Alpha and the future of CX* June 28, 2022 https://www.telusinternational.com/articles/generation-alpha-future-of-cx#:~:text=There's%20a%20new%20generation%20on,strong%20by%20the%20year%202025.

Tootell, H., Freeman, M., & Freeman, A. (2014). *Generation alpha at the intersection of technology, play and motivation.* In 2014 47th Hawaii International Conference on System Sciences (pp. 82-90). IEEE.

Turk, V. (2017). *Understanding Generation Alpha.* Hotwire Consulting: UK. Retrieved from https://www.hotwireglobal.com/generation-alpha

Turkle, S. (2011). *Alone together: Why we expect more from technology and less from each other.* New York: Basic Books.

UNFPA (2014). *The power of 1.8 billion adolescents, youth and the transformation of the future.* The state of world population. Retrieved from https://www.unfpa.org/sites/default/files/pub-pdf/EN-SWOP14-Report_FINAL-web.pdf

Vettorino, Madison. *Here's What Marketers Need to Know About Gen Alpha* November 2, 2021 Https://Inspiramarketing.Com/Heres-What-Marketers-Need-To-Know-About-Gen-Alpha/

Williams, A. (2015, September 19). *Meet Alpha: The Next 'Next Generation'.* The New York Times. Retrieved from https://www.nytimes.com/2015/09/19/fashion/meet-alpha-the-next-next-generation.html?_r=0

Wilmer, H. H., Sherman, L. E., & Chein, J. M. (2017). Smartphones and cognition: A review of research exploring the links between mobile technology habits and cognitive functioning. *Frontiers in Psychology, 8,* 605.

World Economic Forum (2016). *New Vision for Education: Fostering Social and Emotional Learning through Technology.* Retrieved from http://www3.weforum.org/docs/WEF_New_Vision_for_Education.pdf

Woods, Paul. "How to Rev Up Your 5th and 6th Grade Sunday School." Children's Ministry Magazine. Online edition: www.cm-mag.com

Yagel, Gary. Anchoring Your Child to God's Truth in a Gender-Confused Culture, January 1, 2018

Endnotes

Chapter 2

1 Barna Group *Guiding Children to Discover the Bible, Navigate Technology & Follow Jesus How Ministry Leaders & Parents Partner in Faith Formation* 2020.

2 "50% of children will experience an absent parent by age 18 with three out of five mothers of infants working outside of the home, requiring alternative childcare or supervision" Stephanie Kramer, "U.S. Has World's Highest Rate of Children Living in Single-Parent Households," Pew Research Center, December 12, 2019, https://www.pewresearch.org/fact-tank/2019/12/12/u-s-children-more-likely-than-children-in-other-countries-to-live-with-just-one-parent/.

3 https://www.wf-lawyers.com/divorce-statistics-and-facts/.

4 https://sites.dartmouth.edu/dujs/2010/05/30/risk-and-resilience-in-children-coping-with-parental-divorce/.

5 www.Familyequality.org/fbs

6 https://www1.cbn.com/cbnnews/us/2020/june/new-survey-shows-most-americans-and-many-who-identify-as-christians-no-longer-believe-in-absolute-truth.

7 Bell, Valerie, *Resilient, Child Discipleship and the Fearless Future of the Church.* Marceline, MO: Walsworth Pub. Co. 2020, 38.

8 Competing Worldviews Influence Today's Christians, Releases in Culture & Media © Barna Group, May 9, 2017 www.barna.com/research/competing-worldviews-influence-todays-christians/.

9 Hettie Brittz Barna Group *Guiding Children to Discover the Bible, Navigate Technology & Follow Jesus How Ministry Leaders & Parents Partner in Faith Formation* 2020, 26.

10 https://www.politico.com/news/2020/08/13/cdc-mental-health-pandemic-394832/

11 Journal of Affective Disorders in June and it analyzed data collected from more than 350,000 college students across 373 campuses between 2013 and 2021. Quoted by Andrew Mark Miller https://www.foxnews.com/us/majority-college-students-suffering-from-mental-illness-anxiety-depression-rise-study. August 19, 2022.

12 CDC acting Principal Deputy Director Debra Houry, in a press release of the CDC's findings. April 1, 2021.

13 CDC acting Principal Deputy Director Debra Houry, in a press release of the CDC's findings. April 1, 2021.

Chapter 3

14 https://www.barna.com/research/six-reasons-young-christians-leave-church/.

15 Bell, Valerie, *Resilient, Child Discipleship and the Fearless Future of the Church.* Marceline, MO: Walsworth Pub. Co. 2020, 28.

16 Matt Markins, Barna Group, *Children's Ministry in a New Reality. Building Church Communities That Cultivate Lasting Faith*, 2022.

17 Barna, George. *Children's Ministry in a New Reality Building Church Communities That Cultivate Lasting Faith*, 2022, 9-10.

Chapter 4

18 McCrindle, Mark, Fell, Ashley & Buckerfield, Sam, *Generation Alpha. Understanding our Children and Helping them Thrive.* Hachette Australia. Kindle Edition.

19 From 2010 to 2019 — the first nine years of Generation Alpha births — the United States saw educational attainment improve among adults between the ages of 25 and 34. During this time frame, adults grew more likely to hold an associate (8% to 9%), bachelor's (22% to 26%) or graduate (9% to 11%) degree as their highest level of educational

attainment. Not surprisingly, the share of adults who didn't graduate from high school (13% to 8%) and only graduated from high school (48% to 46%) fell during this same time frame.

20 https://www.huffpost.com/entry/generation-alpha-after-gen-z_l_5d420ef4e4b0aca341181574.

21 https://www.pewresearch.org/fact-tank/2015/05/08/ideal-size-of-the-american-family/.

22 Carter, 2016, *Understanding Generation Alpha* Preprint, June 2020 DOI: 10.31219/osf.io/d2e8g.

23 Between 2000 and 2010, the Hispanic population grew by 43 percent, rising from 35.3 million in 2000 to 50.5 million in 2010, accounting for more than half of the 27.3 million increase in the total U.S. population. The Asian alone population grew faster than any other major race group between 2000 and 2010, also increasing by 43 percent, from 10.2 million in 2000 to 14.7 million in 2010. https://www.census.gov/newsroom/releases/archives/2010_census/cb11-cn125.html.

Chapter 5

24 Hudson, Dale *Fertile Soil, See Kid'sFaith Grow and Flourish for A Lifetime*. Dale Hudson www.buildingchildrensministry.com, 2022, 20.

25 Amrit Kumar Jha, *Understanding Generation Alpha,* June 2020, 5, quoting Turk, 2017, Tootell et al., 2014; Williams, 2015.

26 https://inspiramarketing.com/heres-what-marketers-need-to-know-about-gen-alpha/.

27 McCrindle, Mark. *Generation Alpha,* Hachette Australia. Kindle Edition.

28 What does too much screen time do to children's brains?', J. Cross, Health Matters New York-Presbyterian, accessed 11 February 2021. https://healthmatters.nyp.org/how-to-manage-kids-screen-time-during-the-covid-19-pandemic/.

29 https://time.com/3858309/attention-spans-goldfish/.

30 Bedtime Use of Technology and Associated Sleep Problems in Children "Hours of television time has been linked with poor sleep quantity and quality as well. A study of children ages 4 to 11 found that increased screen time was associated with increased sleep anxiety, increased night waking, and increased total sleep disturbance.[9] Studies of pediatric populations have also shown that watching evening television resulted in significantly shorter total sleep duration." National Library of Medicine. October, 2017.

https://www.ncbi.nlm.nih.gov/pmc/articles/PMC5669315/#:~:text=A%20study%20of%20children%20ages,and%20increased%20total%20sleep%20disturbance.&text=Studies%20of%20pediatric%20populations%20have,significantly%20shorter%20total%20sleep%20duration.

31 Further, research shows that children, preteens, and teenagers are using massive amounts of media and those with more screen time have been shown to have increased obesity, reduced physical activity, and decreased health. https://www.ncbi.nlm.nih.gov/pmc/articles/PMC4338000/#:~:text=Further%2C%20research%20shows%20that%20children,physical%20activity%2C%20and%20decreased%20health.

32 https://interestingengineering.com/innovation/generation-alpha-the-children-of-the-millennial.

Chapter 6

33 Michayla White, *Millennial Parents of Faith in a Post-2020 World.* D6 Conference, April 7-9, 2021, https://d62021.sched.com/event/iGXY/millennial-parents-of-faith-in-a-post-2020-world

34 McCrindle, Mark. *Generation Alpha.* Hachette Australia. Kindle Edition. 134-135.

35 'Births, Australia', December 2020, *Australian Bureau of Statistics,* Births, Australia, accessed 15 March 2021. https://www.abs.gov.au/statistics/people/population/births-australia/latest-release.

36 Elmore, Tim; McPeak, Andrew. *Generation Z Unfiltered: Facing Nine Hidden Challenges of the Most Anxious Population* (p. 25). Poet Gardner. Kindle Edition.

37 McCrindle, Mark. *Generation Alpha.* Hachette Australia. Kindle Edition. 36.

38 https://time.com/4913687/how-kids-sports-became-15-billion-industry/.

39 https://onlinemasters.ohio.edu/blog/the-finances-of-youth-sports-in-the-united-states/.

40 https://time.com/4913687/how-kids-sports-became-15-billion-industry/.

41 Elmore, Tim; McPeak, Andrew. *Generation Z Unfiltered: Facing Nine Hidden Challenges of the Most Anxious Population.* Poet Gardner. Kindle Edition, 34-35.

42 https://scholarshipstats.com/varsityodds/.

43 School bans most balls during recess: Smart move or going too far? Kelly Wallace, CNN October, 2013 https://www.cnn.com/2013/10/09/living/parents-middle-school-bans-balls-recess.

44 Amrit Kumar Jha, *Understanding Generation Alpha,* June 2020. Indian Institute of Technology Kharagpur. West Bengal, India. 9.

45 Elmore, Tim; McPeak, Andrew. *Generation Z Unfiltered: Facing Nine Hidden Challenges of the Most Anxious Population.* Poet Gardner. Kindle Edition. 28.

Chapter 7

46 cf. Exodus 10:2: 12:26-27.

47 cf. Deut.11:18-21

48 New Revised Standard Version, Revised English Bible, New Jewish Publication Society Version.

49 cf. Psalm 78:2-7.

50 1 Samuel 1:10-16; 2 Samuel 12:16; Lamentations 2:19.

51 Matthew 21:16; 2 Timothy 3:15.

52 Proverbs 3:11-12; 13:1, 24; 19:18; 23:12-14; 29:15-17,21; Colossians 3:20.

53 Isaiah 7:15; Acts 26:4.

54 Lawrence, Jerry, "*Forming Faith in Families,*" Dissertation presented to Dallas Theological Seminary, May 2005.

55 Jerry Lawrence, 144-5. Barna found a similar result. "Our national surveys have shown that while 4 out of 5 parents (85 percent) believe that they have the primary responsibility for the moral and spiritual development of their children, more than two out of three of them abdicate that responsibility to the church. Their virtual abandonment of leading their children spiritually is evident in how infrequently they engage in faith-oriented activities with their young ones . . . In short, most families do not have a genuine spiritual life together . . . how do parents reconcile the apparent contradiction between saying that they have the primary responsibility for the spiritual development of their children and their practice of dropping off the kids for others to provide virtually all of the spiritual instruction that their children receive? By believing that *because* they are responsible and yet personally incapable of meeting their children's spiritual needs, the best thing they can do is to seek the help of others who are more skilled in spiritual matters. Based on their upbringing and the prevailing cultural assumptions, they believe that their church is the best provider of spiritual nurturing for their kids."

56 Dr. Denise Muirkjesbo, Barna Group, *Building Church Communities That Cultivate Lasting Faith* 2022, 45.

57 Barna, George. *Transforming Children into Spiritual Champions.* Ventura, CA: Regal Books, 2003, 81.

58 Sam Luce, Barna, George. *Children's Ministry in a New Reality Building Church Communities That Cultivate Lasting Faith*, 2022, 30.

59 https://research.lifeway.com/2019/01/15/most-teenagers-drop-out-of-church-as-young-adults/ https://www.barna.com/research/resilient-disciples/.

Chapter 8

60 https://www.barna.com/research/current-perceptions/.

61 www.barna.com/research/current-perceptions/.

62 https://faithit.com/12-reasons-millennials-over-church-sam-eaton/.

Chapter 9

63 https://www.barna.com/research/current-perceptions/.

64 https://www.barna.com/research/current-perceptions/.

65 https://www.barna.com/research/six-reasons-young-christians-leave-church/.

66 https://www.dictionary.com/browse/irrelevant https://www.merriam-webster.com/dictionary/irrelevant https://dictionary.cambridge.org/us/dictionary/english/irrelevant.

67 https://www.cdc.gov/nchs/pressroom/nchs_press_releases/2017/201706_NSFG.htmhttps://www.upi.com/Health_News/2020/05/06/CDC-40-of-US-teens-are-sexually-active/8811588709258/.

68 https://www.pewresearch.org/social-trends/2019/11/06/marriage-and-cohabitation-in-the-u-s/.

69 https://ifstudies.org/blog/is-cohabitation-still-linked-to-greater-odds-of-divorce.

70 Michael Lipka, www.pewresearch.org/fact-tank/2016/08/24/why-americas-nones-left-religion-behind/.

71 Tessa Landrum, www.kentuckytoday.com/baptist-life/gen-z-is-spiri tually-illiterate-and-abandoning-church-how-did-we-get-here/article_ea994828-6cd4-5fbd-8352-496ef3eb9c8e.html/.

72 https://www.barna.com/research/2015-state-of-atheism-in-america/.

73 www.barna.com/research/current-perceptions/.

74 https://resources.gloo.us/knowyourcommunity/cf/ A free resource will help you better understand the demographics and patterns of those living within a radius of your church. You'll get insights into age, income, family, behavioral health, and more.

75 https://www.pewresearch.org/social-trends/2019/11/06/marriage-and-cohabitation-in-the-u-s/.

76 https://research.lifeway.com/2021/12/03/7-in-10-women-who-have-had-an-abortion-identify-as-a-christian/.

77 https://www.pewresearch.org/religion/2012/10/09/nones-on-the-rise/.

78 www.barna.com/research/atheism-doubles-among-generation-z/.

79 https://www.christianpost.com/news/americans-believe-bible-book-of-fables-not-literal-word-of-god-gallup.html.

80 https://news.gallup.com/poll/393737/belief-god-dips-new-low.aspx. The vast majority of U.S. adults believe in God, but the 81% who do so is down six percentage points from 2017 and is the lowest in Gallup's trend. Between 1944 and 2011, more than 90% of Americans believed in God. Gallup's May 2-22 Values and Beliefs poll finds 17% of Americans saying they do not believe in God.

81 Dalia Fahmy, https://www.pewresearch.org/fact-tank/2018/04/25/key-findings-about-americans-belief-in-god/.

82 https://answersingenesis.org/church/sunday-school-syndrome/.

83 https://www.barna.com/research/2015-state-of-atheism-in-america/.

Chapter 10

84 Stephen Covey, *The 7 Habits of Highly Effective People* Sharpen the Saw.

85 DeVries, Mark and Annette Safstrom, *Sustainable Children's Ministry—From Last-Minute Scrambling to Long-Term Solutions,* Downers Grove, IL: InterVarsity Press, 2018, 48.

86 Hudson, Dale, *Fertile Soil, See Kid'sFaith Grow and Flourish for A Lifetime.* Dale Hudson www.buildingchildrensministry.com, 2022, 205.

87 "Seventy one percent of the teacher's we've certified received **no formal training** prior to enrolling in our program." Children's Ministry Academy, Online Certification Program, 2011, http://www.childrensministryacademy/ (accessed March 22, 2022).

Chapter 11

88 Elmore, Tim; McPeak, Andrew. *Generation Z Unfiltered: Facing Nine Hidden Challenges of the Most Anxious Population.* Poet Gardner. Kindle Edition. 366-367.

89 Hudson, Dale, *Fertile Soil, See Kid'sFaith Grow and Flourish for A Lifetime.* Dale Hudson www.buildingchildrensministry.com, 2022, 90.

90 Hettie Brittz, Barna Group, *Guiding Children to Discover the Bible, Navigate Technology & Follow Jesus How Ministry Leaders & Parents Partner in Faith Formation* 2020.

Chapter 12

91 William Damon, "The Age of Obsession," *Newsweek*, October 18, 1999, p. 71.

92 Dan Scott, Barna Group *Guiding Children to Discover the Bible, Navigate Technology & Follow Jesus How Ministry Leaders & Parents Partner in Faith Formation* 2020.

93 Quote by Karl Bastian, *Looking Ahead: Trends in Children's Ministry* 2013 KIDOLOGY, INC, Study by UNC Chapel Hill, Southern Baptist Convention https://www.kidology.org/zones/zone_post.asp?post_id=2964.

94 https://www.barna.com/research/current-perceptions/.

95 National Scientific Council on the Developing Child (2015). *Supportive Relationships and Active Skill-Building Strengthen the Foundations of Resilience: Working Paper No. 13*. Retrieved from www.developingchild.harvard.edu.

96 https://www.barna.com/research/5-reasons-millennials-stay-connected-to-church/ Accessed May 21, 2022.

97 Barna, George. *Transforming Children into Spiritual Champions.* Ventura, CA: Regal Books, 2003, 24. Quoted from EPM Communications, *Research Alert Yearbook,* 2003, (New York: n.p., n.d.) pp. 97-102, 317-326.

Chapter 13

98 Average Learning Retention Rates: Monologue (5%) Reading (10%) Audio visual (20%) Demonstration (30%) Dialogue (50%) Practice doing (75%) Teaching others (90%) www.educationcorner.com/the-learning-pyramid.html/.

99 Charles Spurgeon, *A Book for Parents and Teachers on the Christian Training of Children.* "Come, Ye Children"—Three Admonitions, Chapter 13 London: Passmore and Alabaster 1897.

100 https://www.cambridge-community.org.uk/professional-development/gswal/index.html

101 Beckwith, Ivy. *Formational Children's Ministry: Shaping Children Using Story, Ritual, and Relationship.* Grand Rapids, MI: Baker Books. 2010, 24.

Chapter 14

102 Rob Hoskins, OneHope President, *Guiding Children to Discover the Bible, Navigate Technology & Follow Jesus*, A Barna Report Produced in Partnership with OneHope, 7.

103 Barna Group *Guiding Children to Discover the Bible, Navigate Technology & Follow Jesus How Ministry Leaders & Parents Partner in Faith Formation* 2020, 10.

Chapter 15

104 Sam Luce, *Why Our Children's Ministries Should Be More Like Mr. Rogers and Less Like Disney* May 16, 2022 http://samluce.com/2020/12/why-our-kids-ministries-should-be-more-like-mr-rogers-and-less-like-disney/.

105 Matt Markins & Dan Lovaglia, *The Gospel Truth about Children's Ministry.* 2015 (Streamwood, IL: Awana Clubs International, 53.

106 1 Sam. 2:18; 2 Kings 5:2-4; 22:1-2; Prov 20:11.

107 McCrindle, Mark, Fell, Ashley & Buckerfield, Sam, *Generation Alpha. Understanding our Children and Helping them Thrive.* Hachette Australia. Kindle Edition. 95.

108 Sam Luce, *Why Our Children's Ministries Should Be More Like Mr. Rogers and Less Like Disney.* May 16, 2022 http://samluce.com/2020/12/why-our-kids-ministries-should-be-more-like-mr-rogers-and-less-like-disney/.

Chapter 16

109 Check out www.Grace4Kidz.org for complete Milestone class packages.

110 Beckwith, Ivy. *Formational Children's Ministry: Shaping Children Using Story, Ritual, and Relationship.* Grand Rapids, MI: Baker Books. 2010, 136.

111 Beckwith, Ivy. *Formational Children's Ministry: Shaping Children Using Story, Ritual, and Relationship.* Grand Rapids, MI: Baker Books. 2010, 132.

112 Jutila, Craig., et al. *Children's Ministry That Works!* Loveland, CO: Group Publishing. 2002, 59-60.

113 Beckwith, Ivy. *Formational Children's Ministry: Shaping Children Using Story, Ritual, and Relationship.* Grand Rapids, MI: Baker Books. 2010, 132.

Chapter 17

114 Jutila, Craig., et al. *Children's Ministry That Works!* Loveland, CO: Group Publishing. 2002. 41.

115 "Who is Responsible for Children's Faith Formation." Barna Group, March 19, 2019. https://www.barna.com/research/children-faith-formation/ (accessed April 23, 2019).

116 https://www.kidology.org/tabletalker.

117 Tode, Chantal, www.marketingdive.com/ex/mobilemarketer/cms/news/research/19755.html/.

118 www.eztexting.com/blog/42-unbelievable-text-message-marketing-statistics-will-blow-your-mind/.

119 Tode, Chantal, www.marketingdive.com/ex/mobilemarketer/cms/news/research/19755.html/.

120 Tode, Chantal, www.marketingdive.com/ex/mobilemarketer/cms/news/research/19755.html/.

Chapter 18

121 Fowler, Larry. *Rock-Solid Children's Ministry: Biblical Principles that Will Transform Your Ministry* Bloomington, MN: Bethany House Publishers, 2013, 86.

122 Murrow, David, *Why Men Hate Going to Church.* Nashville, TN: Thomas Nelson, 2002. 38.

123 Murrow, David, *Why Men Hate Going to Church.* Nashville, TN: Thomas Nelson, 2002, 203.

124 George Barna, *The Second Coming of the Church,* Nashville, TN: Word Publishing, 1998, 80.

125 David Murrow, *Why Men Hate Going to Church.* Nashville, TN: Thomas Nelson, 2002. 99.

126 Ron Martin, Evergreen, CO.

127 Fowler, Larry. *Rock-Solid Children's Ministry: Biblical Principles that Will Transform Your Ministry* Bloomington, MN: Bethany House Publishers, 2013, 94.

128 Fowler, Larry. *Rock-Solid Children's Ministry: Biblical Principles that Will Transform Your Ministry* Bloomington, MN: Bethany House Publishers, 2013, 92.

129 https://www.military.com/join-armed-forces.

Chapter 19

130 Matt Markins & Dan Lovaglia, *The Gospel Truth about Children's Ministry* 2015 (Streamwood, IL: Awana Clubs International, 15, 17.

131 https://ministry-to-children.com/childrens-ministry-statistics/.

132 Charles Spurgeon, *A Book for Parents and Teachers on the Christian Training of Children.* "Come, Ye Children"—Three Admonitions, Chapter 13 London: Passmore and Alabaster 1897.

133 Larry Moyer, Evantel, Bad News, Good News.

134 cf. Acts 26:4-11 (Before), Acts 26:12-18 (How), Acts 26:19-22 (After).

135 Facebook post on Children's Pastors and Children's Ministry Leaders.

136 David Staal, *Leading KIDS to Jesus: How to Have One-on-One Conversations About Faith.* Grand Rapids, MI: Zondervan, 2006, 88.

137 www.barna.com/research/atheism-doubles-among-generation-z/.

138 https://blog.penningtonpublishing.com/reading/dont-teach-to-the-lcd/. https://www.seattletimes.com/education-lab/a-reader-asks-if-teachers-

focus-on-students-with-lowest-skills-heres-how-four-star-teachers-answered/.

139 Hudson, Dale *Fertile Soil, See Kid's Faith Grow and Flourish for A Lifetime.* Dale Hudson www.buildingchildrensministry.com, https://www.buildingchildrensministry.com/single-post/something-that-recently-scared-me-in-children-s-ministry.

140 Hudson, Dale *Fertile Soil, See Kid's Faith Grow and Flourish for A Lifetime.* Dale Hudson https://www.buildingchildrensministry.com/single-post/something-that-recently-scared-me-in-children-s-ministry.

141 Charles Spurgeon, *A Book for Parents and Teachers on the Christian Training of Children.* "Come, Ye Children"—Three Admonitions, Chapter 13 London: Passmore and Alabaster 1897.

142 Barna, George. *Transforming Children into Spiritual Champions.* Ventura, CA: Regal Books, 2003.50.

143 Lois E. LeBar, *Children in the Bible School* (Westwood, N.J.: Fleming H. Revell, 1962), 27.

Chapter 20

144 Charles Spurgeon, *A Book for Parents and Teachers on the Christian Training of Children.* "Come, Ye Children"—Three Admonitions, Chapter 13 London: Passmore and Alabaster 1897.

145 Jerry Lawrence, *Forming Faith in Families: A Survey of the Parents and Children of Dallas Bible Church.* Dallas Theological Seminary, May 2005. 150.

146 Larry Fowler. *Rock Solid Kids: Giving Children a Biblical Foundation for Life* Bloomington, MN: Bethany House Publishers, 107.

147 Charles Spurgeon, *A Book for Parents and Teachers on the Christian Training of Children.* "Come, Ye Children"—Three Admonitions, Chapter 13 London: Passmore and Alabaster 1897.

Chapter 21

148 https://www.barna.com/research/six-reasons-young-christians-leave-church/.

149 www.barna.com/research/atheism-doubles-among-generation-z/.

150 www.barna.com/research/atheism-doubles-among-generation-z/.

151 https://www.barna.com/research/six-reasons-young-christians-leave-church/.

152 https://www.barna.com/research/six-reasons-young-christians-leave-church/.

153 Some great parenting video resources include: https://axis.org/ and https://saddlebackparents.com/author/amyk/.

154 Dembowczyk, Brian, *Gospel-Centered Kids Ministry* Nashville, TN: Lifeway Press, 2017. 125.

155 DeVries, Mark and Annette Safstrom, *Sustainable Children's Ministry—From Last-Minute Scrambling to Long-Term Solutions*, Downers Grove, IL: InterVarsity Press, 2018. 192.

156 Charles Spurgeon, *A Book for Parents and Teachers on the Christian Training of Children.* "Come, Ye Children"—Three Admonitions, Chapter 13 London: Passmore and Alabaster 1897.

Chapter 22

157 Psalm 127:3.

158 The healing of Simon Peter's mother-in-law (Mark 1:31), healing a leper (Mark 1:41), raising Jairus' daughter from the dead (Mark 5:41) and feeding over 5000 people from 5 loaves and two fish (Mark 6:35-44).

159 Cf. Mark 8:14-21,32-33; 9:5,32,38; 10:35-45.

160 Cf. Parallel passages: Matthew 18:6-14; Mark 9:42; Luke 17:1-2.

161 Cf. Matthew 24:41.

162 Cf. Josephus, *The Antiquities of the Jews* 14. 15. 10. Grassmick, John D. 1985. "Mark." In *The Bible Knowledge Commentary: An Exposition of the Scriptures*, edited by J. F. Walvoord and R. B. Zuck, 2:147. Wheaton, IL: Victor Books.

163 Swanson, James. 1997. In *Dictionary of Biblical Languages with Semantic Domains: Greek (New Testament)*, electronic ed. Oak Harbor:

Logos Research Systems, Inc. *4624.* σκανδαλίζω (skandalizō), ("scandalize"); VERB. cause sin to. make to stumble; to cause to stumble; give offense to., to fall away; being offended or tripped up that could cause falling away from the right path. to entrap, i.e., trip up (figurative. stumble). Various uses: 1. cease believing (Matt 13:21); 2. fall into sin (2 Cor. 11:29); 3. take offense, be offended by some action (Matt 15:12); 4. cause another to no longer believe (John 6:61), 5. cause to sin (Matt 5:29; Rom 14:21 6. give offense, cause another anger or shock, implying sin will be involved if carried out (Matt 17:27; John 6:61).

164 Newman, Barclay Moon, and Philip C. Stine. 1992. *A Handbook on the Gospel of Matthew*. UBS Handbook Series. New York: United Bible Societies.

165 Mark 1:41, Luke 19, Mark 5, Mark 10, John 4.

166 Ingle, Clifford, Ed. *Children and Conversion*. Nashville, TN: Broadman Press. 1970. 40-41.

167 Zuck, Roy B. *Precious in His Sight: Childhood and Children in the Bible*. Grand Rapids, MI: Baker Books, 1996. 213.

168 Charles Spurgeon, *A Book for Parents and Teachers on the Christian Training of Children.* "Come, Ye Children"—Three Admonitions, Chapter 13 London: Passmore and Alabaster 1897.

169 Cf. Mark 10:13-16, Luke 18:15-17.

Chapter 23

170 Herbert J. Freudenberger with Geraldine Richelson, *Burnout: The High Cost of High Achievement*. New York, NY: Anchor Press, 1981. 91.

171 Barna, George. *Children's Ministry in a New Reality Building Church Communities That Cultivate Lasting Faith,* 2022, 84.

Chapter 25

172 Roy B. Zuck *Precious in His Sight: Childhood and Children in the Bible* Wipf and Stock, 2012, 202.

About the Author

Originally a high school teacher in her native Australia, Janine McNally has partnered together with her husband for many years of pastoral ministry. Janine graduated with a Master of Theology degree from Dallas Theological Seminary and is now pursuing her doctorate at Grace School of Theology. She passionately believes in reaching kids for Jesus and enlightening leaders and parents about Generation Alpha. Janine and Gary have been married for thirty years and live in Jensen Beach, Florida. They are the parents to three grown children: Hannah (married to Kevin), Jonathan, and Jami. She directs the operations of Grace4Kidz, a non-profit dedicated to providing gospel centered resources for children.

About the Organization

Grace4Kidz exists to produce materials for Children's Ministries that are clear on the Gospel. Our priority is that children hear the good news that when Jesus died on the cross, He did EVERYTHING that God requires for us to go to heaven when we die. Statistics show that most Christians trusted Christ between the ages of 3 and 12 years. It is our passion to reach children for Jesus. We also are here to serve, equip and encourage Children's Ministry leaders and parents.

CPSIA information can be obtained
at www.ICGtesting.com
Printed in the USA
JSHW010309030523
41188JS00003B/7